Mysteries

Graham Wilson

Copyright
Mysteries
Graham Wilson

ISBN 9780648311232

Contents

Books by this Author

Arnhem's Kaleidoscope Children – A Memoir
Risk Free – A Novel
Mysteries – A Novel

Old Balmain House Series
Little Lost Girl – Book 1
Lizzie's Tale – Book 2
Devil's Choice – Book 3

Crocodile Dreaming Books
Main Series
An English Visitor – Book 1
Crocodile Man – Book 2
Girl in an Empty Cage – Book 3
Lost Girl Diary – Book 4
Dance of Shadows – Book 5

Prequel
Part 1: Return of the Breaker– Book 6
Part 2: Whirlwind – Book 7

Acknowledgements

Thank you to Nada Backovic for cover design and thank you to Kathryn Moore for substantial editing of the previous version which has greatly improved the writing quality and narrative flow.

This book began as a short story of the same name that I published through a writing group within the Sydney School of Arts and Humanities. In writing this story I envisaged a much larger story behind it waiting to be told. Thank you to other members of this group for their advice on both that short story and on my early versions of this larger story.

Also thank you to many readers who have given input on earlier drafts.

If you want to provide input directly on this story or on other matters relating to my books please contact me by email at grahamwilsonbooks@gmail.com

Chapter 1 – Jim – 1975 – Leaving

The town has organised a pauper's funeral for my mother.

A dozen of us stand around her open grave in the baking sun and listen as the priest mumbles some words over the hole in the ground, something about the life to come and resurrection. I watch as a simple wooden box is lowered into this dry dusty void in the dirt. A woman I do not know throws a posy of wilted flowers onto the casket before two men shovel dry dirt on top.

I'm sixteen years old.

The landlord of our house has avoided looking at me throughout the service, but once it is done he offers his condolences and then, while looking at his shoes, says, "If you'd like to stay in the house I'd be glad to have you. But the rent falls due tomorrow. In the circumstances, I'd like to help you out, but my wife is unable to work with a bad leg, so I must have the rent."

I nod and tell him I understand.

Before I leave, the priest offers me words of hope and reminds me God will look after me.

My mother never talked of God in her final days, only of being tired and in pain because of the cancerous monstrosity eating her from the inside. In the end I think she was tired of fighting a losing battle with it and was happy to die.

I return alone to our rented shoebox house and shove the few clothes I own into a canvas bag.

Until Mum got sick we were happy with our simple life, just us two. Of my father I know almost nothing. My mother simply said he'd been a dropkick shearer who got her up the duff, and that he couldn't run away fast enough once he heard a baby was on the way.

I don't even know his name, whether they met in our town, or where he's gone. It didn't seem to matter. My mother was determined to make a life without him, and everything had been going along smoothly until the big C came to visit.

After that she didn't last long, and the bit of money she'd put away went even faster. She never looked for charity, so we muddled by until it was over.

I walk out into our garden for a last look, the place where I'd picked open flowers that morning to put inside her coffin before they shut her away.

The flower garden was her one delight in the weeks before she died. It's only a small space, three steps long by two steps wide, but all our food scraps went here, along with sink and bath water. Each day, when the sun's heat was gone, she would push a chair beside it and sit there smiling at its colours and marvelling at each bee that buzzed by.

Day by day, she grew thinner and weaker, but she smiled at the garden just the same. In those last days, when she could no longer walk, I'd carry her to sit there. She'd smile still and reach down to pick a flower to put by her bedside.

I hope the smell and smiles of the flowers I put with her this morning will travel with her wherever she's going.

The next morning a neighbour collects me and drops me at the train station in Moree, an hours drive away. I purposefully don't look at the flower garden before I leave for the last time. I know they'll die once the water and care stop, and their death is something I don't want to imagine. One more death following another. More than any other thing, the idea pushes me to leave that day.

The tar is melting as I board the train in Moree, bound for Sydney. My life is before me and, despite my limited start, the future is a place full of promise. As the train comes down off the hills into the Hunter Valley, I luxuriate in the sight of green grass and fat cattle, then as we cross the Hawkesbury River and roll south towards Sydney, I take in views of rocky hills and clear water. Finally, we reach the vast sprawling houses and roads of Sydney. There are so many people with so many cars and other things it's hard to comprehend.

My known world was heat, flies and hard baked ground in summer, cold wind whistling through a freezing house in winter, so how to describe the first sight and smell of Sydney, as seen through a country boy's eyes? Everyone here seems to have so much.

Mum's parting words, whispered to me in a fading voice, float into my mind. "I've done my best but I've nothing of value to give you. You'll have to make a life on your own. Don't expect help from God or any others. They'll only screw you over."

She'd told me to take our last money with me. "It's in a jar beside her bed, fifty-five dollars in small notes. It's yours, all I've saved. I know it's not much, but it's enough to pay for a train fare to leave this accursed town."

My mother had paid the bills by doing odd menial jobs such as cleaning, bar work and domestic help including cooking and childminding for as long as I could remember.

Since I was ten I'd also worked a good bit to add to our finances, at times as a rouse-about in shearing sheds, lawn-mowing when it rained and grass grew, fence mending on farms and the like. I went to school when I couldn't find a good excuse to escape it, and there I learned enough reading and writing to get by and enough numbers to do basic sums and count out change.

But all this starts to become a fading memory as Central Railway Station beckons as the new promised land, I still have twenty five of those fifty-five dollars in my pocket, and I'm old enough to leave school behind and strong enough to do hard work.

It's mid-summer but only half hot. I step off the train, hitch my bag over my shoulder and set off to explore, walking east towards the scent of a distant sea and half known tales of fabled places like famous Bondi Beach.

I don't reach the beach but instead find a big open park, which is a good place to sleep while the weather is fine. Tomorrow I'll find work, something like yard, hotel work or cleaning. Perhaps something in a lumber yard. I'm not fussy, all jobs are equally fine, so I'll search for whichever one best suits my mood tomorrow.

The weeks pass and soon become months. Sydney is now my home and I've slid into comfortable familiarity with the city's inner suburbs, the places I walk through on my way between my many and varied jobs.

I have a hundred dollars in my jar in place of the fifty-five I left home with. I promise myself that, next week,

I'll go and find a bank and put the unneeded extra money in there for safekeeping.

I now rent a share room in a boarding house in Surry Hills with three other young blokes. We're not quite friends, but we keep an eye out for each other's things and, at times, share food. We all work hard and spend little time there. Even though the beds are wire framed and the mattresses are lumpy, it sure beats the park when howling southerlies or rain storms come.

Chapter 2 – Mick – Long Time Past

Mick had lived in Sydney for a few months before it began to feel like home. He'd been shipped there with two other Irish convicts, Paddy and Billy, all of them transported for petty crimes. This and their young age and poor Irish heritage was all they shared in common, yet locally they'd become known as the Irish Brothers.

Mick was serving his seven-year sentence toiling in a work gang in a quarry digging out soft sandstone. It was in demand for the town's new buildings. Apparently the Governor of Sydney, Lord Lachlan Macquarie, encouraged by his wife, the lady, Elizabeth, was said to like making grand buildings from the yellow-brown stone they quarried.

The quarry was around the back of the harbour on the west side of Sydney's semi-circular quay, the main place where big boats docked. Locals called the bay alongside their quarry 'Cockle Bay', on account of its abundant shellfish. Mick often noticed dark skinned women gathering shells from the bay's shallows and selling them to the stonemasons to make mortar to hold their blockwork together.

Even though there was no real kinship between the three Irish men, more and more they chose to work side by side, cutting and handling the blocks, sharing a piece of dry bread or a cup of water, telling a joke to speed the day's passage. As more months passed, they started to watch out for one another, back each other in skirmishes they found themselves in and join up out of work time for a friendly drink.

Their job, every day, was to dig out the stone and cut it into square or rectangular blocks that were suitable for house building. They did it in summer, when the days were hot and the quarry sweltered, and they did it in the winter when a cold wind blew and cut through their thin clothes.

The blocks they cut were mostly delivered by boat, loaded at their own quarry's jetty at the water's edge, and taken to building sites around Sydney. The biggest demand was for the new government stables that Governor Macquarie was building. These blocks were unloaded at another small jetty and ferried by cart up the hill to where they were stacked awaiting use.

Sometimes one or two convicts would go with the boat to help with the loading and unloading of the blocks. It took two men to lift a stone block, as most were more than the weight of a grown man, two feet long, by a foot and a half wide, by a foot thick. They were crafted into a regular size to make building easy, not like the way the masons back home in Ireland worked with the stone as it came, sorting it by size and shape and then fitting all the pieces together until they locked in place in a drystone wall, or maybe with some mortar to make a house.

The boat trip was a sought after escape from the stone cutting drudgery. It offered a couple of hours of lighter labour, so competition for this role was fierce. But the boatman had his favourites who he asked for, and as an Irishman himself, he liked Irish lads. They reminded him of his own beginnings, were light on their feet, nimble, and easy to chat to. That's how the Irish brothers eventually got to make regular trips and, slowly but surely, they got to know the builders working on the new government stables. Mick marvelled at the quality of the workmanship he saw there. No corner cutting was allowed.

The stables was a grand building of stone turrets and arched entrances. People said it would be the grandest building in all of Sydney. It was designed by Francis Greenway, a former convict who now worked for Governor Macquarie. It seemed he'd found the Governor's favour and now his designs were marvelled at across the town for their style and elegance.

Mick heard it said that the lords back home had grand houses like it, with the stone cut square and smooth, but none of the Irish Brothers had ever been up close to the house of a lord in their home country.

Here, in Australia, it was different to back home. Most people worked, that is apart from the soldiers, who swanned around in their peacock outfits of a bright red colour and would often hit convicts without reason. Here the ordinary people were mostly of a muchness, not poor, not rich, just determined to make a new life in this land through hard work and thus get ahead.

Most convicts were like Mick and here for minor crimes so, after their sentence, they would be given a ticket of freedom. Once Mick had that he'd be able to come and go as he liked and work for whoever he chose, maybe even buy a plot of land. Perhaps he could return home, even though home was starting to feel like a fading memory and an impossible dream.

Working on a building for the Governor was a great opportunity. Word was that he was all for freeing convicts and giving them positions within the new colony. Already emancipists outnumbered the free settlers. If he worked hard, perhaps soon his turn would come along, and this opportunity would be his.

After two years their regular boat trips paid off. Paddy turned twenty-one and gained a promotion to a job working for Joe, the master mason, who directed stonework at the rapidly progressing government stable buildings. Paddy's work began with smoothing and dressing the blocks to be fully square and even before they were mortared into place. Joe, another Irishman, was old and grizzled. He liked to give opportunity to kinsmen of his land. Over the next half year, with encouragement from Paddy, Joe found places for Mick and Billy on his building team too.

When the stable building was done, in their fourth year in Sydney, the Irish Brothers stood side by side at the back of the grand opening celebration. All the lords, ladies and others of high class had gathered to celebrate the special day. They agreed it was the grandest building yet built in Sydney.

Governor Macquarie's term was almost up and he was due to return to London, along with his wife, in a few short months. As a parting gift he gave freedom to the convicts who had worked on building his grand stables and government offices. So, one day, a month after the buildings were finished and all the other work was done, the Irish Brothers found themselves emancipated. They now had the freedom to come and go as they wished.

Building in stone was all Mick and the other Irish Brothers really knew, so they decided to continue in that line of work. Many new stone buildings were planned for fast growing Sydney town, and masons with knowledge of building were in short supply.

They were now all well grown men, each with strong arms and hard hands from years of stone cutting, shaping, lifting and mortaring.

For now they rented their own yard behind the docks in Cockle Bay, close to the many quarries that still mined the sandstone. They paid the local blacks to collect seashells for them from the bay shallows, which they fired in a kiln and then had ground into a mortar paste.

After two years, they'd all made a tidy sum and agreed to split the profits and go their separate ways. Billy, the youngest, and an explorer at heart, wanted to ride over the mountains and take up land on the green plains beyond. Paddy, the oldest, had his eyes set on fertile land up north in the Hunter Valley, accessed from the river of the same name, through a new town called Maitland. That left Mick, or Michael O'Flaherty, as he chose to be known these days, to continue his work in Sydney alone. He decided it was time to build his own house, and he had enough saved to cover this expense. There was a good supply of stone blocks in the yard left over from other jobs, the ones not quite square or in need of more dressing.

While he knew he could continue on with this business and prosper, the plans of the others to seek out new horizons had got him to thinking about where his own best opportunities might lie. This town had a great thirst for whiskey and rum. The high prices paid for imported spirit, when added to by government duty, had given him the idea of having his own product as an easier way to make a living than keeping on with his current heavy manual work. Of course, as a business owner, he could now pay others to do much of the heavy manual work, but a day in the hot sun hewing stone was still hard, draining work, and he thought he'd already had done his fair share.

As he chewed this idea over in his mind he formed a view that what may work was a newly located business premises, further out of town, on which he stored the stone and other building materials. By living on site, he could keep an eye on his goods. But, at the same time, he could easily double his income by making his own spirits and selling these discretely to wine merchants to on-sell to their customers. Far easier to let others do the sales to drinking customers; his interest was only that it could bring him good money for a modest effort on his own behalf.

To avoid detection, he needed to do it carefully and not get greedy. He could source the required materials through a mixture of imports and local produce. Both his mother and grandfather were renowned makers of a local poitín in the hills of County Cork that was highly regarded. As a child he had often helped in this work, so he understood the basics, if not all the specifics.

What he needed was a discreet house on the outskirts of Sydney, one far enough away from the daily traffic to get little unplanned visiting, and one built in a place of soft dirt from which he could dig out a basement space large enough for both liquor storage and for a still to do his own brewing. It needed to be cleverly designed to keep it out of sight of any casual visitors or tax collectors. It was intended as a place of production and storage only, not a place of sale.

So, he began to cast around for a place fit for purpose. After a month, he found it, a short mile from the main road to Parramatta and about two miles past the end of the town. This was far enough to discourage casual visitors or the indigent who thought they may find something to steal. As the land was beyond the town limits, with no nearby houses or planned development, there was little interest in it. The soil was poor and ill-suited for crops, and there was no known water nearby for pastured livestock. It was just sandy scrubby land with a mix of wiry grass and shrubby trees.

There was an aboriginal camp a few hundred yards away, within a slight hollow in a patch of shady trees, which he presumed indicated a soak in the sandy soil. This was a good sign for digging his own well for water. And, as far as he was concerned, the nearby blacks' camp was a positive. He'd found the blacks he dealt with to be trustworthy and friendly, though this view was not common among other settlers who spoke ill of them and, it seemed, mostly despised them.

Perhaps it was because he paid the black women who collected cockle shells for him a fair wage that he'd found them good to deal with. He'd grown up poor but honest with parents who taught him to have no truck with rich people who tried to cheat the less fortunate, so he knew he could hardly cheat those working for him and expect them to be fair to him in return.

His overall view was that a nearby blacks' camp would discourage others from hanging around near the site of his own business. Maybe they'd also provide a useful source of labour when required.

He decided he needed to have a title to this patch of land; he reckoned an acre or two would suffice. He didn't want too much land to care for, but he did want enough for a house and stable, along with an outbuilding for tools and open land for stacking stone and other building materials and enough grazing area to pasture a cow for milking and on which a horse could live. Still, he must not let it become too grand, or it would draw hangers on.

He counted out his money and worked out he could pay up to ten pounds for the land. If he applied further out he could get a land grant of up to one hundred acres, but this did not appeal as it was too far away from both his building customers and from potential markets for his spirits.

In the end, he secured two acres for a pound an acre on a ten-year lease. It was on the condition that he improve the land with a house and any other needed business premises over that period, after which he would be able to seek a freehold title. It seemed fair and reasonable, and he was also encouraged that nobody else had sought to buy or lease any land nearby at this stage, though as Sydney grew it would surely come out this way.

Chapter 3 – Jim – 2013 – Discovery-

My house is old by Australian standards. A friend, knowledgeable in older houses, told me its construction features suggest a build date of around 1820, a time when those who came on the first fleet were not yet old. Perhaps it should be listed on the Heritage Register, but it's not grand or in any way remarkable. It seems to have been forgotten about by time.

It sits in an obscure Sydney suburb, not one of the well to do early locations like Balmain, Glebe, Paddington or The Rocks. It occupies a gap between two old and decommissioned railway lines running west of the city, all alone in a no man's land between Newtown and Redfern. It looks like the railway builders knocked down all the other houses around my house when they built these lines. Somehow this one was forgotten. Perhaps a railwayman lived here once to work the signals. If so, nobody remembers his story now. I've searched local libraries, old railway records and many other places, wherever I can think of, but I've found nothing. Nobody seems to have bothered to tell the story of this building.

I also know it's old because it's built of sandstone blocks, one's that look as if they were convict hand cut, the chisel marks on them still sharp, the stones held together with seashell mortar. The roof is slate, except for a front porch with timber shingles, which leaks when it rains.

It's a house of only two rooms, a main room with a front and back door and a small room alongside it, entered from the main room. I use the small room for my bedroom. The main room serves as an office, living and dining room, with an ancient sink and stove in one corner. An outbuilding provides my toilet, bathroom and laundry. It has an old copper boiling tub and a cast iron bath. I think this part was built at a later time.

I've lived here for thirty years. When I bought it, I'd just returned from five hard years of working in outback mines. I carried a pocket full of cash, which the tax office had no business knowing about, and I was tired of being homeless. I needed a place of my own, somewhere to call home. The house's freehold title, which dates from 1933, the depression era, was of dubious provenance, so I bought it with cash for a low price. The real estate agent told me the buildings were a leftover of a long-deceased estate, and there was little interest due to their poor condition and a location wedged between the railway lines. To this day not even lost druggies come here, only mice, weeds and windblown bags find it a worthwhile stopping place.

Thirty years of neglect have not improved the house since I bought it and, while I've thought it deserved a facelift, I've never had any spare cash. Until now.

I've never met my mum's older sister but, when I was about eight, she'd sent my mother a letter. In return, my mother sent her a photo of us together. Somehow this aunt remembered me in her will from all those decades past and, with her death, a cheque for fifty-three thousand dollars drifted into my bank account.

The money won't go far paying builders, but I'm still handy, if getting a bit long in the tooth, so I'll use it to pay for good quality materials and do the building work myself. It's not like I plan on pulling off the roof or other big dramatic fix ups like that. I only plan to strip out the old fittings and put in modern replacements.

Perhaps I'll also create a private back yard within a walled off garden and grow flowers like my mother used to. I have a need to put some fresh daily beauty into my life. It's become a sterile place with only the shells of empty memories in residence. I don't even have neighbours. My home is at the end of a dead-end road that almost nobody comes along.

It's not that I'm antisocial. I have a handful of mates who I meet at the pub for a few drinks. But, as the years have passed, I've become more isolated. I like to think I've grown mostly comfortable in my own skin, but really I'm just lazy about getting to know others. I work odd jobs, just a day here and there, enough to live on and pay the bills. I mostly read old books, a mix of history and mystery. These transport my mind to other places. It's not a bad life. It just seems to have become bleak with the passing years.

An image of Cindy, who I met when I came to Sydney as a teenager, enters my mind. She was like me: another teenager out on her own. We lived together for a year in a one room squat in Woolloomooloo. I was eighteen when our baby, a tiny thing who we called Emily, came along.

But there was barely enough money for two of us, let alone three, so I took a job over the mountains for a month. I left Cindy with all the money I had, two hundred and twenty dollars. It was just enough to pay the thirty-dollar weekly rent for the room and leave a bit for food. Cindy assured me she would be fine. I left her with loving kisses and a pocketful of dreams. I came back a month later with a thousand dollars in my pocket, but Cindy and Emily were no longer there, and our squat was vacated.

A few of Cindy's things were thrown in the street, mouldering in a pile. The man and woman now living in our place knew nothing; the other few people I knew in the neighbourhood also knew nothing. All the landlord could tell me was that a week after I left town, Cindy and Emily vanished too. When the rent fell due it wasn't paid, so he gave our place to another. There were always plenty in need of such spaces.

I searched for a long month, going all over this part of the city, looking in all the places I could think of. But there was nothing to give a clue. Then my money was gone, and I had to leave and find more work.

I went west to the mines, where I made plenty of money. I had hoped to come back to Sydney and look some more for Cindy and Emily, but five years passed by, and five years is a lifetime of empty absence.

There was another special woman for a while, but she grew tired of the loss burning in my heart, and so she went away too and never came back.

Now, at odd times, I enjoy a woman's company for a night. The rest of the time it's just me, in my home, alone. I've got used to it. I feel I've moved past the ability or need to change.

I return my focus to the present and the task ahead of me: the renovation. The house floor is covered in flagstones, old rectangular slabs of sandstone, worn smooth over time. Between them is a mix of sand and dirt with odd remnants of mortar They're cold and damp underfoot in winter, so I plan to lift them and put a dry layer beneath. I begin by photographing them in position, then I number each stone, so I can recreate the sequence when it's time to put them back. My furniture is minimal, so I move it to the back yard and cover it with a canvas tarp to protect it from the weather. I'll live in the outhouse, with my kettle, microwave and bedroll on the floor, along with my chair and books for company, until the work is finished.

I begin in the living room corner furthest from the back door, carefully lifting each flagstone free and stacking them outside. It's slow heavy work and takes two long days until all are lifted and removed. What lies below is interesting but unremarkable, the odd English coin or scrap of another distant past hidden amongst the rubble, but there's nothing buried here to fire my imagination.

I move into the bedroom and continue the floor removal. At first it goes the same, but halfway across the room, I find another block of stone sitting below the block I've just lifted. This block is different. It's square cut and smooth, about two feet each way. I scratch my head and push on. The square cut stones are now a new pattern beneath the old flagstones, and they have me intrigued.

I remove the rest of the flagstones, brush away the loose dirt and look closely. The second layer of stones completely covers one half of the bedroom floor. They look fresh cut, untarnished by use.

I try to lift one free. It's jammed tight, as if somebody has mortared it in place. This is my house's very own mystery. I take a picture on my phone. Perhaps one of my mates will know what the stones could be there for.

It's Sunday and getting late, and tomorrow I'm working in the local lumber yard, so I go to the pub to drink a few knots out of my muscles.

My mates look closely at my phone pictures, and one, an old house buff, says, "You need to let that State Heritage mob know about this. It could be an old grave or buried treasure. Reckon they'll fine you millions if you dig it up without permission."

I'm not a lover of government telling me what to do. But he has a point. I don't want to lift these stones only to find a pile of buried bones.

Of course, treasure's another matter, but that's the stuff of fairy stories, the kind that only happen to somebody else, one first sprinkled in magic dust.

The next day, I ring up the Heritage Office and tell them a bit about my discovery. The person on the phone seems only half interested. She says something about needing an archaeological investigation. I can see all my money fast running down the plughole as a rich dirt digger, one with some fancy degree, gets even richer at my expense.

"Well, I might as well get to work myself and dig it up, see what I find," I suggest. "Perhaps pirate treasure or a body is buried underneath."

This seems to get her interest. "Wait a minute. I'll put you through to a Heritage Officer."

A friendly woman's voice comes on the line. "Kate here, how can I help?"

I give her the potted version. I can tell from her tone she's intrigued.

"How old did you say the house is?"

"The title deeds are from 1933, but a friend in the know says much older, maybe 1820. Despite my best endeavours to find out, it seems nobody knows."

"I'd love a look. Is it possible to arrange a visit?"

I can feel this getting out of hand and want to run a mile. She has no details to let her find me if I hang up now. But there's a musical timbre to her voice that will not let me go. It's a sound that reminds me of another time and place, a long distant familiarity, but I can't bring that memory into my mind to place it.

So, despite my better judgement, I suggest a time and place in two days' time, to meet at a pub on the main road corner in Newtown.

"I don't know about that, I'm happy to meet you at the house if you give me the address."

"The streets here don't make much sense, so it's hard to find. It'll be easier if you follow me there from the pub."

I hear reticence in her voice. "What you propose is outside of normal procedure." But she agrees, despite whatever her reservations.

I like that. Something about her intrigues me.

I don't know what to expect when I meet her a couple of days later, but when I see her from behind, waiting for me on a bar stool, I instantly know it's her.

She's probably in her mid-thirties, and she has brown hair and a trim figure. She pushes her hair back from her ear, a mannerism that feels intimately familiar to me, as if I've seen it before. Her face isn't one I remember from another place or time though, but her smile captivates me.

I propose we have a drink while she tells me about her heritage role, and I tell her about the house, before I take her and show her what I've found. She acquiesces, though I can tell she's impatient to see the house, not talk. I drink a schooner of beer while she sips a lemon lime and bitters.

I begin by telling her about my purchase of the house and its dubious title, then of my inheritance of enough money to do a limited fix up. "I've taken photos and recorded the pattern of the flagstones, so everything will be able to go back how I found it."

She nods. "It is good you have done that. Having a record of the past is always important."

"So, what are the rules before I go further?"

"Let's have a look first."

To pass the time until I finish my drink, I ask her about herself and what led her to do this work. I expect some meaningless answer, but she turns to me and says, "I think it's me trying to find a part of me I'm missing. I was adopted, and my parents are wonderful, but a part of me wants to discover a past I never knew. Maybe that's why I've always been drawn to study old things."

She shrugs. "I know it's not my own past when I research old buildings, but it's still a way of me being connected to what came before, to build a story of a past that I can put myself inside."

I nod, unsure how to respond. To cover my non-reply I quickly finish my drink and suggest she follows me in her car. In five minutes, we're there.

"Well, here it is. It's not much, but it suits me okay." I invite her inside.

Her eye for detail is amazing. She's already pointed out ten things that tell of the house's early history as we walk through the door and go inside.

"Your friend was dead right about this being from the early 1800s. I can't understand why it's not listed on the national estate.

"It's clearly one of Sydney's oldest houses."

I take her into the bedroom and show her the mystery of the stones I've uncovered. She looks at them from all sides and walks back and forth, closely studying them. "This is remarkable. I wonder why they're here?"

She kneels down and studies them minutely. "I'm looking for quarry marks or things to identify them," she tells me. Just as quickly she seems to forget I'm here, appearing oblivious to my presence, her mind far away, lost in total concentration in her work.

As she bends forward to look more closely, a small silver pendant falls out of the front of her top, swinging free on its silver chain below her neck. She stands and turns towards me, eyes alight with something important to tell me that she's just discovered.

But my mind is unable to hear her words as she enthuses to me. All I can see is the pendant hanging from her neck. It has the name 'Cindy' in connected silver cursive letters, mounted on a silver base.

I reach out and turn it over. On the back, in faded inscription, is a heart symbol and the words, 'From Jim'. My head reels and I stagger backwards.

She reaches out to steady me, concern on her face. "What is it? You look ill. Are you okay?"

I can only point; my words have run away.

I remember so clearly the day I bought the pendant. It was only a couple weeks after Emily was born. I didn't have money to buy Cindy a wedding ring, or pay for a wedding. Our wedding was a thing of promises, not anything official. But the extra twenty dollars I'd saved bought this, and I gave it to Cindy with all my love. She shyly accepted it from me and allowed me to hang it around her neck, where it stayed until she went away. Now it's returned into my life.

Kate is looking at me, puzzled. I still haven't spoken. Instead, I take her hand and lead her across to the mantelpiece above the stone fireplace. On it is a black and white photo, in a plain frame, of a young woman and a tiny baby. It's the only photo of Cindy I have. It remains my most treasured possession.

Faintly glimpsed on Cindy's neck is this same pendant, detail indistinct, yet its outline clear. I point to the pendant in the photograph and then to the one hanging from Kate's neck. "How did you get this?"

But she's staring at the woman, oblivious to me and my question. At last she says, "I don't know. I was found abandoned outside a hospital when I was a tiny baby. The only thing on me, apart from my clothes, was this." She touches the pendant.

I pick up the photo and hand it to her. "This is Cindy. I think she may be your mother."

Chapter 4 – Jim – Ghosts of the Past

I'm standing looking at this slip of a girl who must surely be my daughter. Her name is Kate, but if she was an abandoned baby wearing the pendant I gave to Cindy, it must surely mean she's Cindy's child and my daughter, my long-lost Emily. No wonder she has some familiar looks and manners; they are those of her mother, still burnt sharp in my brain after more than three decades.

But now what do I do? It must be a huge shock for her to find out this way, and maybe she hasn't yet understood my role. She's well spoken and presented, obviously highly educated; she clearly comes from a stratum of society far above my own.

I must look decrepit to her, a man well into his fifties who does odd jobs and whose schooling was over at fifteen, while she's a university top achiever. Should I admit my role in her parentage, or leave it as an untold story, say that I knew her mother, that one day both mother and baby vanished and I, a friend of that distant time, have never known what happened. Perhaps it is even crueller to leave her with only half the story.

I need to know the circumstances of her discovery; this may be the only way I'll ever get some clue as to the fate of my Cindy, the person who has left a hole in my life that's never been filled.

As these varied thoughts flow through my mind, I realise she's still standing here with tears in the corners of her eyes, silent and unmoving, gazing at the woman in the picture with a naked, unquenchable hunger.

After a long minute, it seems her brain computes that I must have some significance to have known her mother. She looks at me with piercing eyes, ones full of questions and uncertainty. "Does that mean… How is it that you knew her? How do you have a photo of this woman with my pendant who you say is my mother?"

The only way forward is to begin with the truth, whether it's easy or hard to hear. "The pendant was Cindy's. I gave it to her in place of a wedding ring just after you were born. You were our baby. I had it engraved with a love heart and my name. One day you and your mother vanished. For over thirty years, I've never known where you went or what happened to either of you."

Now she's the one looking faint with shock. I find her a seat, and she sits with her head resting in her hands, quietly shaking her head from side to side, as if in confusion.

This day has been a huge shock for me. I think it's even more so for her, finding the first fragments of a beginning which has eluded her all her life.

I cross to the kitchen and put the kettle on. There's nothing like the ritual of tea to buy time and portray a semblance of ordinariness. "Will you have a tea?"

She nods, offers me a tear glistened smile. "Please. Milk and one sugar."

I make it and carry it to her, my hand shaking. She drinks her tea the same way Cindy took it.

She takes it, her hand shaking more.

I collect my own tea and sit on the chair beside her. We sit in silence, sipping our tea, each processing our own thoughts, neither knowing how to advance the moment.

At last she says, "I'm sorry. This is hard for me to comprehend. What you're saying is that you were, you still are, my father?"

I nod, finally manage to say, "I think I must be."

Slowly our words begin to flow, and I tell Kate how I met her mother, of our brief bonded togetherness, of the birth of our much-loved daughter, Emily.

"We talked often about building a future together, of having our own house and raising a family that nobody could take away. Both of us had already lost too much before we met. That's why I just couldn't understand where you'd both gone when I came back home. I had enough money to rent our own flat, just the three of us. I would have married her formally. I'm sure we'd have had more children in time. I thought that's what we both wanted.

"No matter how hard I searched, I couldn't find either of you. It got too painful to carry on searching, finding nothing. I'm sorry I stopped looking for you both. I had to get away from here and the memories, so I went to WA to work. It was five years before I came back. By then it was too late."

"I really wish you hadn't stopped looking," she says without malice.

I tell her again of those endless days of pain and empty searching and how it grew too great. I don't tell her that part of me believed Cindy must have left me for another and didn't want to be found.

"I wish I could tell you more than I already have. But I only have fragments of knowledge," she says. "After I was found outside the hospital I was fostered for two weeks until my parents adopted me. No trace of my biological parents could be found.

"I want you to know though that my parents are good decent people who've cared for me and loved me ever since. I've had a happy and prosperous life. They've always told me the truth about being left at the hospital, and they've helped me try to trace my birth mother lots of times."

She makes no mention of them searching for a father, and I feel a sense of loss that she never actively tried to find me. My mind tells me this is unreasonable, but it's like the other elephant in the room — she has yet to really acknowledge who I am other than a connection to her mother. Still, the talking together is building bridges to the past, and I'm clearly a part of that past too.

After a while, we've told each other everything we know of that time, and our talking seems to reach a hiatus. I know I could ask more of her parents of today but, somehow, I don't want to. To acknowledge them further seems like building on the loss of a daughter who has never known me. In fairness, I owe them much for all the care they have lavished on my daughter.

Kate equally doesn't ask me more about myself. It seems that this room is full of elephants that neither of us wants to see or acknowledge.

When our tea is finished, I take the cups away, rinse them and say, "Well, you came to see a house. You should tell me some of what you discovered today before I interrupted about the pendant and the picture."

She looks at me directly for the first time in a while. "I'm sorry, it's been such a shock, and I have so much to absorb. I think I need to leave telling you about the house for another day, if that's okay. I really want to tell my parents about meeting you first. Perhaps we could meet again tomorrow?"

She goes over to take a last look at the picture.

"It's the only copy I have, so I couldn't bear to lose it, but you're welcome to take it with you today, show it to your parents, get a copy made."

She nods her thanks and I ask her if she'll find her way back from my house. "Yes, thank you. I'll remember the way." She holds out her hand and lets it linger in mine. She has fresh tears in her eyes. "I know you're my father, but my mind just cannot compute it yet. Please give me time to understand. And thank you for your kindness today and for telling the truth. This is the start of something."

I find I have tears in my eyes too and can only nod.

Almost as an afterthought, she leans over and kisses me on the cheek. Then she is gone, and all I have is the faint perfume of lost presence.

Chapter 5 – Mick– My House

It's been a month since I bought my block of land. It's spring and has rained since I bought it. All the trees are amass with flowers and twittering birds, which seems an auspicious sign.

I recently paid two of the blacks from the nearby camp to help me dig a well. Their English is small, but we get by with hand signals and gestures. As time goes by, we start to share words for common things.

They tell me they are Gadigal people, and one man is a nephew of that well-known man called Bennelong who travelled over the ocean with Governor Phillip. They've already shown me their soak, an excavated hole into a dry creek bed, which could be called a Native Well. It's a place the whole clan guards protectively. They only allow me to take one bucket of water from it each day, and I understand why; water in this dry country, coming into a hot summer, is something very precious and must be conserved.

My own well is a priority and it's far enough away not to interfere with theirs. One of the men is obviously a water diviner of sorts, a bit fey. When we first made our plan, he spent a couple hours with a fresh cut forked branch, holding the two thin ends in his hands as he waved the other end over the ground, while he walked around. I understood he was waiting for the stick to twitch as it was drawn to water. When he finished he took me to a place in the back corner away from their camp where he indicated we should dig.

The ground where he suggested we dig is in a slight depression with some big trees around it, which provide good shade. Maybe trees are a sign of water. He indicated we should find water at five or six paces below the ground level, which I infer means fifteen to twenty feet, a manageable dig for three people over a couple days.

Unlike the soil where we plan to build my house, which is of a light sandy texture, this soil is heavy, beginning with loam and soon becoming grey clay with red ironstone flecks. Even if there is nothing else down there, the clay we dig out may become a useful render for parts of the house. We also use some, as we dig, to bind the well's sides together, making it less prone to collapse as our hole gets deeper.

By the end of the first day, we've dug to a little below head height. This feels like good progress though the ground we dig remains dry. The second day's digging is harder and has become slow as we now have to lift out the dirt we dig with a rope and bucket. By the end of the second day, we've passed two head heights in depth, making the lifting heavy. Still the ground remains dry. I worry that we've chosen the wrong place for the well, but the water diviner remains confident. He says the next day we'll find water.

Sure enough, by lunchtime on day three, there is an ooze in one corner of our well. By mid-afternoon, we're down to a depth where there is a good flow of clean, clear water, which tastes sweet.

We cheer and clap exuberantly as the water flows out in a solid stream.

We dig out another two feet of dirt to make a good space for the water to fill, deep enough to fully drop in a bucket. The final day's work is to square off the top with bush timber, make a cover to keep rubbish or animals out, and fit a windlass above so we can wind up water a bucket at a time.

I'm so pleased with our success I give my workers extra shillings plus a bag of flour for their labours. I'm confident we've formed an alliance to protect this place against other intruders who might seek to help themselves in my absence, and that I've found a future source of labour to assist in the work I plan to do.

The next week I peg out the site for my future house. As it's only for me, it does not need to be big or grand. I think two rooms and an outhouse will suffice. The first room will be an all-purpose room with a stove and fireplace, a table and chairs, a bed in one corner and some shelving to stack food and other household goods. The second room will be entered from the first. It will have a heavy padlock on a door, for which only I have a key.

To any who ask I'll tell them it's my secure storeroom to keep safe the things I value. At a casual glance it will appear like a plain store room, but beneath it will be the place where I brew and store liquor. Its existence will only be of known by a trusted few. We'll only begin to build the underground space once the outside shell of the house is finished, as this will hide our inside work from view.

I've chosen this place for my house because the sand is soft and dry. I hope it will remain dry for a good way down, without buried rocks to seriously impede my excavations.

My first job is to bring the unused blocks from my other work yard at Cockle Bay, which I've kept as my main business premises for now. I own a heavy dray pulled by two horses and each day, in the following days, I give a task to two labourers to load this dray with the sandstone blocks, bring a load to my bush block, and stack them in place ready for building work to begin.

After two weeks I have a good pile of stone and am ready for my building work to begin.

We have a small party on site to celebrate the beginning of my home, and the next day I get to work with my two new working companions.

My secrets are likely to be far safer with them than with my other workers, in part because they have so little English and in part because they do not associate with others who may pass their stories on.

Chapter 6 – Jim – Meeting Cindy

Four months have passed since I arrived in Sydney. It's not so hot now; summer is fading, and the leaves are changing colour and falling from the English type trees, ones different to the scrubby gum trees and mulga of my hometown. It's fascinating to see so many new different things around me.

I've made friends with a young bloke called Robert, who works as a gardener in Centennial Park, the place I first slept when I arrived here. He studied at a place called Sydney University doing a thing called Botany, and he also has friends who work at the Royal Botanic Garden who know even more than him. He gets me occasional labouring jobs in both these places.

The pay is poor, but the wealth of knowledge of these people fascinates me. I ask them the names of things they grow: oak trees, maple trees, and the like, as well as giant fig trees, which they assure me are from my home country. My income falls away, but my at least my mind is filling with new knowledge, which it seems to absorb like a sponge.

I've moved out of the boarding house in Surry Hills as I've been allowed to camp in a back room in one of the huts at Centennial Park. In return, I do out of hours work to keep the park secure at night, locking the gates as dark falls and doing an evening walk around to locate any vagrants and deter thieves who would steal or damage our things.

There are a couple of old alcoholics I turn a blind eye to, but I discourage those who think a good time is to smash windows, shoot roosting birds or throw wild night-time parties. I don't play the brave hero, but often just a shout or shining a light will suffice to make people vanish.

During the day I'm learning other skills, like how to drive the machinery: tractors, ditch diggers, mowers, and other things. I don't much care about my wages; my rent is free, and I get just enough to pay for food and occasional night-time entertainment.

Every couple weeks, Robert invites me along with him to visit Kings Cross, where he hangs out with friends, has a few drinks and listens to music at the local bars and nightclubs. I've rarely spoken to girls before, whereas he has many female friends and also some male friends who seem to like other boys. It's all part of my life education.

I discover I'm naturally quiet and not interested in anything too wild, and anyway, I have limited money for drinks, and certainly none to pay for girls of the sort he sometimes goes with to their beds. The idea that people pay others money for an hour or two of sex is something I'd never conceived of.

I'm too shy to even talk to the hookers, as he calls them, or any of the richer girls he associates with. Still I enjoy women's friendly smiles and occasional flirting glances. They seem to promise more if I knew what moves to make next.

In time I settle into being a known person in these places. Now the security guards and barmen treat me as a friend, and some of the girls give me a friendly hello when I pass by.

I've been in Sydney for over a year and a half and am approaching my eighteenth birthday when I first notice her. She's a street girl who makes her money by selling her body. She's less flirty than some of the women I've met around Robert and his friends, so I feel more comfortable with her. Her name's Jo, and she looks about my age. Gradually, we begin to say hello, and then strike up small conversations as we pass each other by.

After a couple months of small conversations, she sees me and catches my eye one night. She waits until I'm alone before she approaches to say hi. We make small talk for a minute before her tone becomes more serious and she says, "I'm off work at two tonight. I wondered if you wanted to come by when I'm finished. Maybe we could just hang out and see what happens."

I'm not quite sure she means what I think she might mean, but she's sweet and pretty and she makes me feel comfortable around her in a way no other woman ever has. I'd love to get to know her more even if nothing happens, so I say yes and return at her finish time.

For a while, I'm on my own, but eventually another of her friends, who I've briefly glimpsed in passing before, walks over and sits next to me. "Jo sent me with an apology for not being here. A client's booked her for the rest of the night and she can't come."

I'm disappointed, but I smile at Jo's friend and thank her for telling me. When I stand to leave she looks at me with a timid expression and says, "You're welcome to hang out with me for a while instead. It seems a shame you coming here for no reason."

I look at her closely. Her dark hair is tied back to expose a fine swan like neck, and she has a lovely figure, but her face is what captivates me, those eyes seem to see into my soul. They reach within me and wrap around my heart.

I feel a bit breathless as I ask, "What's your name?"

"Cindy," she replies.

I hold out my hand. "Jim."

Her soft hand grasps mine. Her delicate perfume flows aound and over me.

So, it begins.

I get the idea that Cindy is a prostitute too, but I don't ask her directly. Instead, I ask how she came to find herself in this part of Sydney.

"I'm not going for the sympathy vote or anything. No need to feel bad for me. I just want to answer your question honestly. I grew up in foster care after my mum died from an overdose when I was little. I went to a few different foster families over the years, then when I was twelve I ended up with a foster father who thought he'd visit me in bed in the middle of the nights, if you know what I mean."

My expression must be shocked because she looks at me and says, "No sympathy. It's long ago now."

"I'm sorry that happened to you."

She acknowledges my comment with a nod before continuing. "I ran away at thirteen when I realised my foster mum knew and would do nothing to stop it. That's when I came to this part of Sydney. Since then I've earned money selling my company. Sometimes I've had to sell drugs. At least it's all on my terms now."

I'm amazed how open and honest she is with me. For the first time since I've left home I feel I've met someone like me, someone else struggling to make their way in an often hostile world.

An hour passes and then another as we talk and talk. Finally, it's five o'clock and the street sweeper disturbs us, making us move away from where we sit on the gutter at the side of the road.

"I'm sorry I've kept you so long," Cindy says. "Jo told me you were really sweet. Now I've spent time with you I can see what she meant."

We both pick ourselves up and I'm about to offer to walk her home when she says, "I hope you don't think this sounds too forward, but if you'd like to come back with me to my room I'd love to spend some more time with you. Not as a client, just as us together." She takes my hand, as if to lead me, her eyes questioning.

I don't know what to say to her. Her suggestion isn't anything I expected. In the end I say, "I've never talked to someone as much as you, and you are very beautiful, so I'd be lying if I said I didn't want that. But do you think we could talk some more and try being friends for a little while before we do anything more?"

Cindy gives me a radiant smile that warms all of my insides from end to end. She kisses me on the cheek and says, "Yes. I'd love that. I'll be working here again until about midnight. Perhaps we could meet then."

Somehow, I know, at that moment, that I do want to be with her, but I also know I don't want her to do this thing anymore with others.

"How about we go for a walk in Centennial Park today after you've had a sleep. I live and work there. I'd love to take you to see it."

Cindy takes my hand again. "I have a better idea. Why don't I go there with you now, and we'll walk together in the early dawn before we both sleep."

So, we walk, sharing the new dawn light together, and then we sleep in my room at the park, our bodies entwined in exhaustion.

We wake in the mid-morning and lie there dreamily for an unknown time.

She rolls towards me and moves her body partly over mine, her face on my chest and nuzzles into me for a long minute. I stroke her hair and hold her close.

"I love the feel of you lying there," I say.

She unbuttons my shirt and runs a fingernail over my bare skin, and then slides it down over my belly, sending thrills all over me. Then she puts her mouth over mine and gives me a long and intimate kiss.

She whispers in my ears, "Did you like that?"

I nod, it was beyond words.

She takes my hand and places it over her breast

God how I love the feel of her, so full and womanly.

She moves my hand down lower, encouraging me to explore the rest of her body. Every part of her feels utterly delicious and I push my body over hers.

She pushes away for me for a brief instant and I feel cheated. But she stands and unclips her top and skirt, now wearing only lacy underwear.

She pulls me to my feet and undoes my last shirt buttons then my belt and pants and pulls the last of my clothes to the ground. "I wanted to see all of you," she whispers, touching me with finger tips that send shivers all over me and make me mad with desire.

She looks up, dark hair framing her beautiful face, "Now you can finish undressing me."

We make love. It seems to go on forever and the ecstasy is overwhelming. After a short break, bodies still joined, we make love again then sleep.

By the time we wake again it's lunchtime, and we're both starving. We catch the bus to the beach and sit looking out over the waves while we eat hamburgers. It truly seems like the good life.

For a while we play chasing waves before we walk to the furthest end of the end of the beach and sit on rocks at the bottom of a cliff. It curves around and rises up sheer against the ocean. It seems like we stay for only minutes, but I know it's many hours as we talk and talk.

As the spring sun begins to fall behind the headland, Cindy, suddenly conscious of the time, springs up and says, "I must go. I have to be back to shower and get ready to start work at six."

The thought of her going off, doing with strangers the beautiful thing we've done together with our bodies, tears at my heart. I don't want her to have to share herself with another. I want her to be mine and only mine. I hold onto her hand and say, "If you never had to go back and work there again, would you?"

"I don't know how else to make money to survive."

"You could stay here with me. I know that together we can somehow find a way."

So we talk some more and finally agree it's something we both really want to do, no matter how poor we are or how difficult it might be.

In that minute, I know I'm already in love with her.

For long while, we stand in the fading beach light, holding each other.

Survive we do, though it is hard.

The first night, she rings in sick, but next day she says she needs to be honest and let them know she's leaving. She says she'll go on her own, but there's fear in her expression.

I take her hands and pull her face close to mine. "Please let me come with you? I couldn't bear the idea they might try to force you into staying or might even hurt you."

She nods her agreement.

My worries are correct. Her pimp comes out to meet us and tries to bully her into staying and me into leaving. But I have no fear of him. My hands are hard and my knuckles are scarred from all the years when I had to learn how to fight to survive in a country town. We stand toe to toe for a long minute as he eyes me off in an angry way, as if to say Cindy belongs to him.

I stand still, keep my stare direct and make my face stay calm, refusing to respond to his threat.

After a while the Madam walks up and pushes him away. She brings us into an office and sits down, makes up Cindy's pay and puts it in an envelope. "I'm sorry to lose you, Cin. Come back if you change your mind."

The money will help us begin our new life together.

Cindy moves into my room at the park, but Robert soon makes it apparent it isn't acceptable for a couple to live there. There isn't enough space.

We search for and find a room in a big old house at Woolloomooloo, not far from the places Cindy knows. Through her past contacts, she gets work cleaning rooms in hotels, and I carry on with my usual range of odd jobs. I know I need better wages, but Sydney is in a downturn, and jobs have become scarce over the last six months. It's no longer easy to find casual work; there are often morning queues of people looking for odd jobs at hotels, building sites and other likely places.

When I first met Cindy, she had been a drug user. Not a full-on addict, but needing a regular fix to get through her days and nights. She's determined to quit so the money spent won't become a road block to us being together. An organisation called The Wayside Chapel organises two weeks in a drug rehabilitation Centre for her so she can have a serious go at kicking her habit.

The two weeks feels like an eternity without her, but then she's back out and we're together again. We work on finding lots of things to do together that help keep her well away from temptation.

We briefly talk about the idea of us moving to the country where, in return for me doing farm work, we would be given a house to live in and some food along with a small wage, but Cindy says she's a city girl who has only known that life. Being out in the middle of nowhere would both terrify her and send her mad with boredom, so Sydney will remain our home.

She does go with me a couple times for a week at a time when I get work shearing in sheds over the mountains, but she finds the life of a shearing worker's wife to be lonely and, after that, she doesn't come away with me anymore.

She enjoys the freedom of being able to get work in the city making up hotel rooms or doing kitchen work in the bigger hotels in the Cross, so that's how our life together rolls along. Until Emily.

We've been together just over six months when we find out she's pregnant. Since she left her job at the brothel, we've become lax about contraception.

Both of us love the idea of having our own child. It will be the start of a new family we'll create and raise together in love and security.

Money remains an ongoing challenge and, as the time for the baby grows closer, there are new expenses: doctors' visits, baby things to buy, the list goes on.

We live hand to mouth, pooling whatever we earn and avoiding all luxuries. When Cindy is six months pregnant, I propose and she says yes. We plan to wait until after the baby is born for a proper ceremony so we can both keep working and saving money for as long as possible and so skip the cost of the ceremony for now. She also tells me she doesn't want photos with her with a protruding tummy on her wedding day. As my mother was never married, I don't worry too much. I just want to have things done right for Cindy's happiness and for the happiness of our child.

Cindy says she finds it hard to think why I'd want to marry her with her bloated belly, but to me she's the most beautiful thing I've ever seen, and I tell her so, which makes her laugh. We may not be financially rich, but we're rich in other ways and utterly happy together.

She has to give up work when she's seven months pregnant; her regular hotel says they can no longer give her work, and her doctor also advises her to pull back on the physical work. She's diagnosed with something they call pre-eclampsia, which makes it very high risk for her and the baby if she keeps working, so mostly she has to lie down and rest.

This doesn't spoil our delight being together and watching our child grow and move inside her belly. We lie side by side on our narrow bed for hours, my hand resting on her bare belly, both of us getting a thrill when our baby kicks and moves about.

When her waters break, I take her to St Vincent's Hospital where, eight hours later, I see and hold our baby daughter for the first time. We name her Emily Rachel. Cindy has an idea that Emily was her mother's name, and Rachel was my mother's name, so it seems to fit perfectly.

Life gets even harder when Emily comes home. We need extra food for Cindy to make enough milk for our baby to grow. As our money is so tight, I agree to take a month's work during spring shearing season at the shearing shed I worked for last year. My expenses will be low, and I'll save all the money for us that I can. When I come back, we'll have enough of a deposit to rent our own house. Despite the personal sacrifice, we agree the work and temporary separation is a good idea if it gets us a place of our own.

Cindy recovers well from the birth and seems happy and settled with our new baby. She tells me that, while I'm away, she'll get work back at the hotel she worked at before Emily was born. They've agreed she can bring Emily with her as she works, and this will help pay the bills while I'm away. I don't love the idea. I've been promised a small cottage on the farm if I'll work for them over the spring, but Cindy won't agree to come along. She's worried about snakes and wildlife now we have our baby, and she wants to earn and make her own contribution. She says the hotel work will give us more money than the savings in not paying rent.

Reluctantly, I agree and I go and she stays. I promise her I'll come back on the weekend after the fourth week with the money I've saved. Then we'll go out together and find our own place to rent.

My last remembrance of her is seeing her with tears glistening in her eyes as she waves me goodbye from the front door of the house where we stay. It's a bright sunny Sunday afternoon, and six-week-old baby Emily is in her arms. I say my last goodbye and give them both a hug before I walk off down the street. I turn for a last glimpse of her and Emily at the door.

Then I turn the corner and walk on, with no sense that I'll never see her again. I walk on to Central station, from where I catch the train and travel over the mountains to Bathurst. A farmer I know meets me off the train from Bathurst, and he brings me the half hour drive to begin work on his farm the next day.

There is no phone where I am and no phone in the house I share with Cindy. But that night I write her a letter, then it is two. Work is busy, and I never go to town. Instead, I work all the days for more money.

My letters to Cindy sit there unsent. Would they have kept her there until I returned if I'd sent them?

Chapter 7 – Jim – Looking, Looking

The month I spent searching for Cindy and Emily when I returned to Sydney has faded into a blur.

It was getting late on Friday afternoon as I got off the train, my pockets bursting with cash, me half walking, half skipping as I made my way to our home.

If I could convince Cindy to return with me, the farmer had offered Cindy work at the farm house, a mixture of domestic work and child supervision, paid at a fair rate, along with our own cottage to live in. It had a flower and vegetable garden and was built down by the river, which ran out of the mountains. It could be ours for as long as needed. He was holding the offer open for a week before he looked for someone else to fill it.

That day, I felt rich beyond measure with all the good things of life: a wife, a daughter, the promise of more work and our own home to live in at no cost, as well as my thousand plus dollars.

I stopped at a flower stall and bought a bright bunch of flowers, a 'Spring Special' the seller called it, along with a bag of lollies for Cindy's sweet tooth.

As I approached the front of the house, I noticed a few things piled on the kerb outside and felt puzzled when I recognised some of Cindy's clothes amongst them. Perhaps she'd done a clean out, though I was surprised to see some of her better clothes in the pile and couldn't imagine she'd no longer want them now she was back to her pre-baby size. But I was impatient to see Cindy so didn't think too much about it. Instead, I opened the front door and strode down the passage to our own door, expecting to sweep Cindy off her feet and shower her and Emily in hugs and kisses. I banged on the door and called out. At first there was silence, then a shuffling sound. It wasn't her light-footed walk.

The door part opened. A thin faced, almost weasel looking man, peered around the part opened door and asked in an unfriendly voice, "Who are you? What do you want?"

I'd never seen him before and was sure he wasn't a friend of Cindy's. His rudeness was puzzling. He was smaller than me. I could easily push him aside if I wanted. I forced myself to be civil. "I was going to ask you the same question. This is my place. I live here with my wife. Can you get her for me please or, if not, then please step aside?"

An ugly scowl came over his face, and he stepped directly in front of me. "Who the fuck do you think you are? This is my place, so you can fuck right off."

I couldn't see into the room, and my fuse was growing short, so I pushed him aside and stepped past him. A slovenly looking woman was sitting in a chair. There was a bed in the place where ours had been, but I saw none of our furniture or possessions I recognised and no sign of Cindy or Emily. I stood, open mouthed, staring in amazement.

Finally, after an uncountable time, I realised the man and woman were both pulling at my arms, trying to get my attention and talk to me. I think they realised I had much bigger issues to deal with than fighting them over possession of a rented room.

It turned out they'd lived here for a fortnight, having moved in at the weekend two weeks after I'd left. All they knew of the previous occupant was this person left a week before they moved in. They knew nothing about any clothes and other things belonging to my wife, which were now piled in the street.

The woman said, "Those things were there in the street when we moved in. I think some of the best bits have been taken by others but some still remain. I really wish we could tell you more, but that's all we know."

I thanked them and apologised for barging inside, then I went to the landlord's room and banged on his door for ten minutes. He didn't answer, but eventually another resident came out of their room to see what the commotion was about. I'd never seen him before and he knew nothing about my Cindy or Emily; he'd only moved in a week ago.

I realised we knew almost nobody in this place, that for the time we'd lived here we'd kept almost completely to ourselves, fully wrapped up in our own lives and with little concept of others who shared the house with us.

My only contact with the landlord was to give him the rent money each fortnight. In fact, Cindy normally paid him, so I barely knew what he looked like.

Still, I had to do something, so I went from door to door, determined to keep at it until either somebody answered or I was convinced that nobody was there. After knocking on all but one of the doors of the other rooms, I finally found someone home who responded, a middle aged woman with a friendly smile, who said, "How can I help?"

I said, "Hello, I'm Jim. I have been away in the country for a month and have just come back. I am am trying to find my wife and baby who were staying here when I left. Her name was Cindy. I am wondering if you knew her at all or remembered seeing her recently?"

She replied, "Of course, the pretty dark haired girl with the little baby. I spoke to her a couple times and once, when her hands were full with shopping things, I held the baby while she unlocked her door. That time she introduced herself and told me her baby was Emily. Apart from that we waved to each other or said a passing hello a couple times.

"The last time I saw Cindy was about three weeks ago. I remember because it was that cold rainy day, and lovely little Emily was dressed snug as a bug. I didn't keep her talking long because she seemed preoccupied with whatever she was going out to do. She had Emily in her pram. I didn't want to interrupt her day."

The woman is a motherly type who seems trustable, so I tell her more about Cindy and Emily being gone and ask what she thinks I should do. I'm at my wits' end and panicked as to what to do from here.

She invites me in, makes a cup of tea, then gets a pen and piece of paper and writes list of suggested places to try.

"The landlord normally gets home about six, and I'd start with him. Not that he's much use as a human. I don't fancy your chances of him being any help. I saw him dumping a pile of clothes on the street, but didn't realise they were hers. I don't know what he did with your furniture."

I ask, 'Can you remember what day it was when you saw them, you said it was a rainy day?"

She nods and thinks for a few seconds. "Yes, it was a Monday, that was the last day it rained. It came after a lovely sunny weekend, the one almost three weeks ago."

"So they went out on the Monday morning and you have not seen them since?" I confirm.

"Yes, I'm sure I'd remember if I had. And I know the clothes were put out on the street before the next weekend"

I realise that Monday was two days before our next rent payment fell due, and from what the people now living in our room have told me, they moved in that next weekend. So it's clear the landlord didn't wait long before acting."

I thank the lady for her help and say, "I will go and wait for the landlord to come home."

I sit on the door step to wait for the landlord. It's late before he comes, but I am prepared to wait all night if needed. He must have stopped off at the pub because he stinks of beer and walks with a swaying motion.

His manners are as bad as my mood, which has been going south each hour that passes. I am scared at what could have happened to Cindy and Emily and angry the landlord has treated our possessions with such little respect. We'd lived here for more than a year, far longer than most tenants. It seems reasonable to me he'd at least have kept our things in storage even if he rented out the room again.

As I accost him at the front door, he doesn't even recognise me at first. "What the fuck do you want?" he asks when I stand to meet him, putting my body between him and the entrance door.

He tries to push past me to go inside, muttering a curse as I obstruct his path.

I have no patience left for his rudeness.

I grab his arm and reef him to face me, pushing my face a few inches from his. "I want to talk to you, dickhead. If you try to walk away again before I finish, I'll knock you onto your arse and kick the fuck out of you, so try it if you want."

This seems to break through the fuzz in his brain, and now he looks at me properly, but still without recognition. "Okay, settle down. No need to be nasty. Why don't you tell me what you actually want?"

"I'm looking for my wife and baby, Cindy and Emily. I've been away working for four weeks, and I've returned today to find them gone. You've rented our room to someone else and tossed our stuff in the street. I want an explanation. It better be good if you don't want to end up spending the night in emergency with a smashed up face."

Now he looks at me closely. "Oh, I see now, you're the guy who was with her with the baby. One day here, next day gone. I figured you'd shot through on her, decided a missus and kid was too much work, that it spoiled your fun.

"Well, she only stayed a week after you left. Then one day she up and offed with the baby in a pram. I don't know why, but she was heading off with a purpose, not going for a stroll. I reckoned she'd shot through too, maybe gone back to her old life on the game. That's what I figured.

"And I must have been right because, sure enough, she never returned or left a forwarding address for her things. I didn't want them, just junk really. I left them in a pile on the kerb where anyone who wanted bits could help themselves. Most of the best stuff has gone. I was planning to put the rest in the back of my ute and drop it at the tip this weekend, but now you're here you can do me a favour and get rid of the rest of it yourself."

As he speaks the anger fades away from me. Sure, he hasn't done right by her or me, but it is nothing. All that really matters is that Cindy is gone. The idea she might have gone back on the game or gone with another man feels like a physical punch. I thought I knew her better and I don't really believe it and yet, once he spoke those words, it is hard not to believe them without a better explanation.

It feels like she'd purposely waited until I was away and then returned to an easier life, one which certainly paid better than any other jobs she or I have had since we met.

I believed she loved me. We had a baby together, and I'd never seen any shadows to our happiness. But still they are gone and it feels like a part of me has been ripped from my body. The half-smile Emily gave me on the morning I left was pure joy, and I ache to see it and her small face again.

In the end, I just walk away from him, devastated.

I sit on the kerb alongside the refuse of our life together, too numb to even cry. I just sit there, unmoving, and stare at this small pile of things, the only remnant of my family.

I must have sat there for hours, because the traffic is gone and the street is deserted apart from odd bats flittering shadows in the streetlights when I feel a hand on my shoulder. It is the woman who'd been kind and made me a cup of tea. She pulls my arm, takes my hand and leads me inside her room. She sits me at her table and puts a plate of food in front of me. I have no appetite and yet, at her urging, I eat, a mechanical process. She folds out her lounge, lays a sheet and blanket on it and indicates it is my bed for the night before she turns out the light.

Her name is Margaret, and for a week she helps me follow the list she's written. We go together to the houses along the street and ask the people who answer if they know Cindy or know where she and Emily have gone. After that, we visit everywhere else we can think of, one place at a time. We have our list and cross places off it as we go.

Neither of us has a car, so mostly we walk, other times we catch a bus or train and sometimes a taxi. We go to all the local police stations, hospitals, churches with priests, brothels and hotels. We knock on doors, and we ask passers-by and business owners. I take my only photo of Cindy and Emily with me to show to people. The picture shows Cindy holding baby Emily in her arms. It was taken the second weekend after she came out of hospital. We paid to have it taken in a photoshop in Kings Cross on that magical day I'd proposed, given her the pendant and she'd said yes. I still think of that day as when we really started our life as a family together.

People we show it to look closely. It seems some vaguely remember Cindy from before she met me. She had lived around here for two or three years before that time. But nobody remembers seeing her in the last month, and certainly nobody has seen Emily.

After our first day of searching, Margaret tells me to bring inside the things left in the street and sort through them. She takes all the clothes and washes them while I sort through the rest of the things. There is very little of value, most is meaningless junk. But there are a couple of picture books and some baby things I keep, not that I know what use they could ever serve. In the end, we jointly select a rattle Cindy and I bought for Emily, and couple of other small baby toys, which are a link to Emily. I also keep the notebook in which we'd both written our plans for the future, and a travel book of places we'd looked at together and decided that one day we'd love to visit.

Margaret folds up Cindy and Emily's clothes and puts them in the bottom of one of her drawers. "I'll mind them for you, Jim. But they're yours and they are here anytime you want them back."

We visit everywhere we can think of by the end of that first week and find nothing at all. In my heart, I believe Cindy has deliberately left me, gone off with another man, a richer man who can give her a good life in some far off place. Margaret never says it, but I think she thinks so too.

At the start of the second week, Margaret goes off to visit her daughter down the coast at Wollongong. "Look after yourself and my room while I'm away. When I get back we'll keep searching, maybe revisit some of the places we've already been just in case we missed something.

"Try hospitals and police stations further away from here while I'm away. You never know."

I do as she suggests, but it is a half-hearted effort on my part because by now I've lost faith in discovering anything, and each empty visit only adds another layer of pain. By the third day my efforts have almost ceased, and I find myself sitting in the park where Cindy and I first walked together in the early dawn, then on the rocks at the beach where we'd sat together on our first afternoon. I remember that magical time as unshed tears cloud my eyes.

When Margaret returns, we revisit all the places we've been in the first week. What we find is the same but for one thing. Outside the brothel, I see Jo again. I ask her whether she has any idea where Cindy has gone. She turns to walk inside when she sees me, pretending not to have heard me.

I run after her and grab her arm before she can reach the door, pulling her around to face me.

"Please Jo, Cindy and our baby, Emily, have vanished while I was away in the country. I need to know where they have gone. Can you help?"

"I want to know as much as you. She's been my closest friend for a long time. But, as you say, she just vanished. If you find anything out will you let me know? I'm so worried about her too"

There is something in her manner I don't quite believe. It isn't that I think she knows where Cindy is now, her face seems honest about this, but it is as if she has some small piece of hidden knowledge, perhaps something Cindy told her from before that she doesn't want to reveal.

She tries to pull away again, but I hold on, saying, "Jo, please, surely you must know something, have some idea. Please help me, I am going crazy trying to find them."

"Truly I would tell you if I knew, but I really don't."

She turns her face away, pulls free and goes inside.

I stand there feeling gutted.

At the end of the third week, Margaret said, "I think you'd do yourself a kindness by going and finding a job in some faraway place. Staying here will only bring more hurt. We've searched all we can."

I know she is right; there is nothing further I can do here. But still I persist for ten more days, travelling ever further afield, asking and looking wherever I go. Nothing comes of it; it's as futile as all my other searching.

Early in the fifth week after my return, I know I must leave Sydney and the endless pain of its memories while I still have the means.

I use my remaining savings to buy a one-way plane ticket to Port Hedland, a town in Western Australia. I'm told there's big money to be made working in iron ore mines.

It's sad to say goodbye to Margaret; she's been the truest friend. But there is nothing to keep me in Sydney any longer.

With a promise that I'll write to her every month, and she to me, I depart. I wonder if I'll see her again. I have lost too many good people from my life.

Chapter 8 – Jim – Far Away

I take a flight from Sydney to Perth, and then, after a half night's stopover, I board a daybreak flight to Port Hedland, along with a crowd of mostly miners, people who live in Perth and fly up and back for a couple weeks work at a stretch. They seem a friendly crowd, full of banter and camaraderie with that sense of excitement which comes from knowing a week of hard work and harder play lies ahead, along with the odd twinging regrets of goodbyes to southern based families, girlfriends and the like.

I sit next to a bluff red-headed bloke that the others called Blue. He is a mine machine driver at a place called Newman, a big mountain of red iron dirt, is how he describes it. He listens to my cut down story about Cindy and Emily and my search. About how I had to get out of town and might as well try and make some real money while I do that.

He gives me a nod and grunt before saying, "Well, I know they need dump truck drivers and ground workers at the mines and blokes in the sheds fixing the machines. If you want to come out to Newman with me, I'm sure I can get you a job, and you can sleep on the lounge in my donga until you get a place of your own if you like.

"Mandy, my girlfriend, won't mind. She's pretty easy. She works as a barmaid and stops over some nights. Maybe she'll try to fix you up with a friend of hers, one of the new girls in town. She likes to line them up with decent blokes, not let them hook up with some of the animals around."

The offer is tempting, but I want to give myself a day or two to look around town and get the feel of the place before I commit to a job. "Thanks for the offer, but I want a couple days in Hedland first to work out what to do."

Blue nods. "Sure. Probably do the same myself."

As we shake hands at the airport before going separate ways, he says, "Well, if you do make it to Newman, look me up. Brian Hayes is the proper name, but near everyone in town calls me Blue Dog, partly on account of the red hair, partly as they reckon I'm like the town's blue heeler dog, snapping at their heels if they get in my way."

"Thanks again, Blue. I'll be sure to look you up."

In the end, I get a job at Karratha, a mining town a couple hours down the road. Hedland has plenty of work, but the town is flat and barren. Karratha is a prettier town, ringed by red broken hills where the iron ore has come to the surface. Up and down the coast from it are scores of pretty beaches where the fish fall onto your line, which makes a good break for a day off.

Following Blue's idea, I first get a job in a machinery shed, though not one for the mines, which are inland. Instead, I work for the railways servicing the mines. The trains haul the iron ore hundreds of miles to the coast. I learn how to service the rolling stock; ore trucks with their wheels and bearings, big diesel engines powering the locomotives. The trains haul ore on carriages beyond count, an almost continuous ribbon moving from mines to ships.

I begin as not much more than a spanner and bolt holder to the qualified mechanics but, with an aptitude for this work, I pick it up quickly. Soon I'm entrusted to undertake major work tasks by myself, largely unsupervised. There is a continual shortage of tradesmen with qualification tickets, so it pays to be a fast learner and, before long, you can get promoted from general dog's body to a job of greater importance and far better pay.

It's two months later when I'm living in workers camp near the port at Dampier that I get asked to accompany a train to the mine town of Tom Price, which is hundreds of miles inland at the top of the mountain. They're having problems with a faulty train shunting system. As we have the same system here, they want someone who knows how it works to have a look and see if the problem is easily fixed. If not, they'll fly a top mechanic out to do the work.

I'm delighted to be offered the trip; it's my chance to see the wider country, and who knows what work options may exist up at the Tom Price mine.

The day after I arrive, I pull the shunting gear apart and soon spot a minor problem: one of the lock mechanisms is fitted incorrectly allowing the connector to come open under load at key times. It's easy to fix and, by the end of the day, I'm done. I spend the next day testing it under operations to ensure it's now working fine. It's perfect, and I'm planning to catch a ride back to the coast when my boss back there radios me and tells me to take a day off and have a look around the town, if I want to, before I ride on the slow ore train all the way back to Dampier.

Mount Tom Price is one of Pilbara's original mines, though new deposits are being discovered every day, so it's the main source of iron ore that heads down to the coast from the Hammersly Mines operations. A small town has sprung up alongside the mine to service it. It has a school, a health centre, a few shops and a hotel.

The head railway mechanic, very pleased I've solved his problem, offers to take me for a tour of the town.

"Well Jim, you've done us a big favour sorting this out so quickly. Why don't you come for a spin with me, see what's around this town, then I will buy you an ale."

"Sounds good to me," I say.

As we drive we chat.

"Seems like a good place to live and work," I offer.

"You're not wrong, good money, plenty of work, a few years here has set up lots of my mates for a new life. And it's funny how many get hooked on the place, and end up staying on and on, not knowing how to leave."

"What about getting a job in the mine itself, servicing or driving one of those huge dump trucks or diggers?" I ask.

"I can put a word in for you to get one of those jobs, if you like, maybe to begin in the workshop which services them. It'll give you an understanding of the different machines used. If you do that job well, it's only a matter of time until you get a job on the mine site in either a digger or dump truck.

"I'm having a drink tonight with the mine's maintenance shed boss. How about I put in a good word for you then?"

"Yes, please. I'd really appreciate that."

Next morning, he has good news for me. "There's a job that's yours if you want it. All you have to do is go round there today to sign the papers. Then, once you catch the train home tonight, you can make arrangements to return and start back here in a couple of weeks' time.

"Wow," I say, "that's brilliant. I owe you big time!"

It's three weeks later when I return. This time I come on an aeroplane with my few things, and the next day I start work for Mount Tom Price mine in the maintenance shed where we fix the mine's machinery.

It has diggers, huge dirt shovel loaders, road graders, and rock crushing machines that turn the massive lumps of ore blasted loose in the open cut mine into coarse gravel material, which eventually finds itself on a train to the port in Dampier where ships come to transport it to Japan. My favourite work is repairing and maintaining the huge tip trucks that carry the lumps of blasted ore to the processing plant for the mine.

One of my job's is to take off and change the tyres of these massive machines. The wheels are twice my height and the tyres and rims are so heavy they need their own machine to lift them on and off. I drive each truck into position for the work to be done, and the feeling of power sitting in a cabin so far above the ground is truly amazing.

Soon I get to know the blokes who drive them on a daily basis. They're a wild crowd. From them I find out how to enrol for driver training. It takes me a month to schedule it and another month to complete the training, but once I've got my dump truck driver ticket, my name is added to the list of rostered drivers.

Soon my job is to be out on the side of the mountain in one of these gigantic machines, feeling the earth shake beneath me as the truck rumbles its way along with a massive load of red ore rock on the back.

I settle into work on the mine and am part of the mine worker's village, a separate place to the main town. They give me a room in a row of huts called 'demountables', one of many in a massive block.

It has a single bed, a small table and chair, a bar size fridge, a wardrobe and a bookshelf. On the wall hangs an air-conditioner which shakes and shudders but mostly blows chilled air over me to reduce the burning outside heat, often above forty degrees. It's made up with clean sheets by a domestic worker once each week. The bed is hard and narrow, with only room for one body, still, it's amazing how many girls sleep over with some of the blokes in similar beds.

There is a large dining room where our breakfast and evening meals are served. We collect our packed lunch on the way out to work each day. There are also communal showers and a large recreation room with a TV, pool tables, books and magazines, a sound system and other things to provide relaxation. The on-site bar runs from six to nine each night, though the limit on workdays is three beers per worker, as they want us to be fresh for the next day. They're not really joking when they tell us the equipment is too valuable to be wrecked by drunks, and driving a huge machine on a sloping road around the side of a hundred-foot hole in the ground is perilous at the best of times.

So, while not luxurious, we each live comfortably with all our basic needs supplied. Most nights we retire early, as breakfast is served from five thirty and work starts at seven to beat part of the baking heat. We work a standard ten-hour day, six on and one off each week. If there's a big push to get more ore out for a ship coming, we often have our hours increased to twelve hours daily, though one break day a week is normally still insisted on. A nominal charge is made for our food and board, but it's so minimal that it has no impact on our earnings.

Half of the workers are long-term stayers and half are fly-in-fly-out workers who come up from Perth for a fortnight before they fly home for a week off. Us stayers can take extra days off if we choose by marking days on the roster, but mostly we keep on working and earning the big cash.

At first, I have no other interests but work, and money pours in. I don't like nights or days off. They give me too much time to think. Instead, I borrow books from the recreation room and use these to try fill my few vacant hours. I have little taste for TV watching, pool games, cards or things other people do to fill in time. I find idle chatter tiresome, and most company is a bore with endless talk of girls or football.

Even so, gradually, I build up a group of mates. Typically, on a Saturday nights, we head to town for a big blow out in the local hotel, free to keep on partying until late, knowing that we don't have to get up for work the next day. I usually drink slowly to keep a clear head. I have no heart for getting drunk and maudlin; it only makes me think about Cindy and Emily and feel sorry for myself, which is a bad mind space. But the Saturday nights at least serve as a weekly marker which put a sense of progress into otherwise stationary time.

Most Sundays, I attach myself to a regular group heading to a waterhole in the rocky hills where we swim and fish for the afternoon. I've bought a fancy fishing rod and, even though I mostly catch nothing, I find fishing relaxing. Some days, I head off along rough tracks through the hills, which run for miles, and walk and walk in the blazing heat, looking out into the shimmering haze, punctuated by odd green tree gullies. Far, far above is a washed-out blue sky. I find, in some strange way, walking for hours in this landcape soothes my jangling nerves and dulls my aching emptiness.

They say time is a great healer. My personal time rolls on, and it feels like nothing changes for better or worse, so instead I try to survive by living in the moment, occupying my mind and hands with things menial and mundane.

I befriend a blue heeler dog that hangs around the camp. Some nights, as I read, he lies alongside me on my narrow bunk bed. I take a measure of comfort in his wordless contact and wagging tail. His silent companionship helps me live through my solo life.

The dog reminds me of the Blue, my one-off flight companion, who I haven't seen since that first day. Like the dog, he carried a persona of predictable stability that reassured me.

After six months of working, I have enough cash in a rapidly growing pile to be able to buy and run a car, so I take a week off and head down to Geraldton. It's about a thousand miles away and is the nearest proper town.

A truckie gives me a lift from the mine in return for sharing the driving, and we arrive a day later. For two nights, I treat myself to Geraldton's best hotel. On the third day, I cruise car yards until I find a lightly used four-wheel drive. I spend half my savings to buy it.

On my return, I pass through Newman and decide to take Blue up on his offer to look him up if ever I'm in town. It's good to have somebody who passes as a friend in this out of the way place.

Blue and I settle into a bar and trade life stories. He tells me how his wife left him for another bloke, how she took the kids and most of the money and, to escape the hole in his life, he came up here. "I traded in my family life for an occasional night with a woman, and now there's Mandy who is sort of regular, though she wants more which I'm not so sure about. The rest of the time I enjoy my own company. That works well for me. I'm almost comfortable in my own skin after the last five years of living like that."

It doesn't sound like much consolation, but it beats my life now, hands down. I feel Blue is like a fellow traveller on the same path through life, so I share more of my own story with him.

"What you need is a night between the sheets with a good woman," he says when I've finished speaking. "Someone who's happy to say goodbye next morning, but who likes you enough to see you again if you ask. Why don't you let me set you up with somebody for the night? It'd do your mental health a world of good to forget your problems for a night."

Part of me knows he's right. Grief gives no answers, nor does grog. But the thought of trading Cindy in my bed, even if only in my dreams, is not a thing I can begin to comprehend yet. So, I thank him politely and move the conversation to safer spaces.

That night, he gives me a blow-up bed on the floor of his room to sleep on, and in the morning I say farewell with a promise he'll visit me at Tom Price before too long. As I drive away, I'm happy to have made at least one friend in the middle of this godforsaken place.

Driving along a rough dirt road on the way home, I notice the outside country in all its spectacular brokenness for the first time since I came to this land. I see a landscape full of red hills, eagles wheeling in the sky above, yellow bleached grass, olive coloured trees, and wallabies that jump out of the way when surprised.

On this drive, I'm more alive than I can remember being since I came here. The earth is not quite green, the sky's not quite real blue in the blazing sun, nor is there a sweet scent of flowers on the breeze, but today brings an essence of a lost life that I've missed without knowing it since Cindy left.

I see a sign for a waterhole and on impulse drive up to its deserted side, a deep hollow nestled in brick-red hills. I plunge my body deep into its icy water. This intensity of cold, sitting alongside the blasting outside heat, brings long forgotten parts of my body alive. The feeling of something real settles over me. It's not peace or happiness, but it's something. Anything alive beats endless emptiness.

Blue and I form a ritual of meeting monthly. I'll visit him in Newman one month, the next month he'll meet me in Tom Price. We have a night time reunion at a bar, with booze and conversation, which seems to work for us both. Usually, at two or three in the morning, we stumble back to the place of whoever is housing us that night and the visitor sleeps on a blow-up mattress on the floor.

Gradually, we expand our meeting circle to have gatherings with work colleagues and friends, but our friendship always sits at the heart of these times.

Chapter 9 – Jim – New Life in the West

Sometime late in that year in Tom Price, Blue tells me he wants me to come, next weekend, to a surprise party he's throwing for a friend. He says it's someone I know, but he won't say who. "Just come to our regular bar in Newman for seven on Saturday." He won't give more details.

Despite my curiosity, I don't think too much more about it until I walk to the bar thinking I'll enjoy a drink and feeling glad to be part of this celebration for another. The door to the bar is festooned with balloons and a large banner that reads, 'Happy Birthday, Jim!"

Someone with the same name as me, I think. I wander inside, and everyone stands and claps at my entrance. Finally, the penny drops.

I do some quick counting and realise I'm twenty-one tomorrow. Someone must have found out and taken it upon themselves to spread it around. Of course, it's on my driver's license, so I suppose it's no great secret.

I've never had a birthday party or any other special occasion in my honour, perhaps a cup cake and a few lollies with my mother when I was little, and there was always a present for each other at Christmas. But parties and celebrations were not something we did, neither was a visiting a church or any religious festival. My mother considered all religions as beneath contempt. She barely spoke of these things, but when she did, there was no hiding her disgust with religion and its people and practices.

She barely spoke of her foster family who abused her and treated her as an inferior servant either, but I have a suspicion they were good church going folks.

I look around the bar and am amazed and moved by this kindness. Blue smiles and pats me on the back. "Happy Birthday, buddy. Enjoy yourself for a night. You deserve it."

As the night moves along, each person drops over for a chat, and as they leave, each passes a gift my way, things like a cap with the motif for the football team I support, new fishing lures, or a bottle of premium malt whiskey. I grow steadily drunker as we cut the cake, hold birthday toasts and drink rum chasers.

There are a smattering of girls at the gathering, some who are friends of friends who I recognise. As it becomes early morning a pretty lass with a bewitching smile is sitting on my lap. Her name is Beck.

Despite my befuddled brain, the feel of her body pressing into mine is wonderful and arousing. She must realise her effect as she wiggles her bottom to rub against me and pushes herself harder into me to heighten my arousal. Once it is obvious she has my attention, she takes my hand and puts it over her breast.

When the party is over, she brings me back to her room and undresses me before she gives me her body in a way that feels so good and right. As I look at her hair-framed face in half light, I almost imagine she is Cindy returned to me. That imagining is balm to my soul.

I fall in to a deep dreamless sleep, the first in untold months where I don't dream of Cindy or Emily. I wake in the early morning to feel Beck's naked body pressed against mine. She is still slumbering, and as I look at her from behind, once again for an instant, I feel Cindy has returned, the likeness from some angles is so strong.

When she wakes and turns to face me, the difference in her features is obvious, although, in that moment, I think her no less beautiful.

We make love twice more before she says, "Though I could stay here all day with you, sadly, I'm going to have to ask you to leave. I have an appointment soon."

"Can I see you again?"

She smiles and kisses me on the nose. "Blue told me your heart needed mending, and I think it's so. I hope our time together has helped in a small way. You're a nice fella, Jim. Call me anytime you're in town."

She writes her number down and hands it to me.

Nothing will ever mend the pain I feel about losing Cindy and Emily but, after that night with Beck, the pain seems more bearable. When I return to Newman a month later, I ask her to dinner. Afterwards, we go to bed again.

After our lovemaking, I cup her face, stroke her hair and kiss her. "I love the time that we spend together."

"Well, I love it too."

"I see myself loving you more and more over time."

She sits up and looks at me with a kind expression. "I feel what you want, and I like you very much, but I can't return those feelings. Each moment we share is a treasure, but it can't be more than it already is. If you spent time with some other women you'll find I was something you needed at this time, but I think you'll find I'm not as special as you think I am. I should introduce you to my single friends to help you understand. You could enjoy a night with any of them just as well as one with me."

So it is, after that, that once a month, on a visit to Newman, I enjoy a night in bed with Beck. Other weeks, back in my home town, I spent time with two of her friends she's introduced me to. Beck is right. It isn't love, but it satisfies my needs and helps me move on.

One of Beck's friends is Patsy. She is a woman of ambition. One night, when I come to her room, she is reading a book, not a cheap trashy romance novel of the type the others I knew favour, instead it is a big weighty tome with a hard cover.

"Reading anything good?" I ask her.

As she goes to set it aside and give me her attention, she looks temporarily embarrassed. I seek to see the cover but she puts it face down to hide it from view.

"Come on, show me. I promise I won't laugh if you show me whatever it is."

Reluctantly, she turns it over.

"Astronomical Physics, Wow, that's nothing to be ashamed of. It's amazing. I knew you were smart."

"I'm studying a part-time degree in Physics with a major in Astronomy through a university in Perth. They send the assignments in the post, and I use the local library when I need text books for the course. It's cheaper doing it this way as I still earn plenty of money here in town while I study. Jobs are easy to get here."

We fall to talking rather than lovemaking. I think both our minds are hungry for a wider world.

After that we meet once a week at the hotel restaurant to share a meal and talk astronomy. As time goes by, we walk out amongst the stars to make observations. Patsy has bought her own telescope, which we set up at times and places where the heavenly views are best.

Her dream is to be an international physicist, travelling the world and studying stars. She has bright lights in her eyes when she speaks about it, as her face burns with her dream.

She's saving money and, next year, she hopes she'll have enough for a year's full-time study in Perth to finish her degree. Then the world will be her oyster.

Our relationship morphs into something much closer to friendship than love. We share a passion in a quest for knowledge. Perhaps she's a little sweet on me, and I'm more than a little sweet on her, but I know I can never compete with her dream, and there is no space for me in that place.

Over months we share dreams and passions that take us to new places. Patsy's a great cook who teaches me culinary skills as well as an appreciation of new tastes and ingredients from other parts of the world, She also has fashion sense and seeks to cultivate this appreciation in me too.

But most of all she is just good company, full of ideas and a knowledge of a wider world which she shares and, as she does, my world expands too.

When the end of the year comes around, Pasty does her sums and works out she can pay for at least six months of full-time study. She's confident she can find a job in Perth to supplement her earnings if needed.

So she enrols as a full-time student and, a few weeks after Christmas, we say our goodbyes. "There's always a free bed and warm body to keep you company if ever you come to Perth, which I hope you will one day."

"I hope so too," I say, although somehow I know our paths diverge from here.

I find I miss her more than I'd reckoned in the days after I watch her jaunty wave as she boards the departing plane.

In the weeks that follow, I am a bit low and bored. At first, I think I am lonely. Patsy has filled up a very large part of my life for months now. Soon, I realise it isn't just the space Patsy has left, it's also a hunger for new knowledge that she's ignited in me.

Once again, Blue comes to the rescue as I pour my heart out to him on our next catch up. He has wisdom beyond his years and, by now, is as much a mentor as a friend. What I most like is his lack of soppy sympathy. He listens for a while then says, "Reckon it's time for you to get off your arse and do something about it, Whingeing won't fix it!"

"Sure, but what do I do about it?"

"Jim, you're not thick, in fact you're even medium smart. But, at times, it seems you act too dumb to see the nose right in front of your face. Patsy did what lots up here do. She used her free time to learn. She studied something that interested her and will let her build a better future, to get paid a real crust to do something that fires her brain. I know you like driving dump trucks for now, but do you want to still be doing it in ten years, if not longer, when you're thirty-something? Then add on another ten years and you'll be forty-something. Is that the life you want?

"You're hiding away from the world here, trying to mend a broken heart. True, I am sort of doing the same. But I've had my family. My kids are growing up, my wife has moved on and I can no longer find the energy to hate her. She's even invited me to Perth next Christmas to spend time with the kids, maybe take them to the beach and the movies.

"Not that we'll get back together, more likely I'll hook up steady with Evie. Since Mandy and I split we've been seeing each other a lot and we've talked about how we might buy a farm down south together with money we're both saving, somewhere down around Margaret River, a place with green grass most times. Maybe we'll have some pets, chooks and horses, maybe we'll even have another kid or two together. It's a half plan of sorts.

"But you, you have no plan. It's time to get on with your life, follow something that makes your heart sing, and I'm not talking about a girl. What I mean is find an interest and learn about it, study it, do courses, get books, do whatever it takes to build your own new dream and start going there."

"But—"

Before I can say any more, Blue puts up his hand. "Don't ask me; just use that thing in your noggin. It surely knows the right answer."

For the rest of the night we talk no serious words, just football, fishing and chasing women, our three favourite pastimes. But I don't forget his advice. He is right. My life is up to me from here.

Chapter 10 – Jim – New Passion

Blue has given me the idea of finding an interest and running with it, at first learning all about it and then becoming an expert, and he has told me it is my job to do this. I can see he is right, that nobody else can look inside my brain and know what I should do.

When he left that night, his parting words were, “Don’t worry about the answer just yet, let it bubble away in your mind and one day, when you least expect it, the answer will come. What I find most helps me to get answers, when I don’t even know what the questions are, is to go for a walk in the late afternoon, not really thinking but just walking and looking around, enjoying the view. Often the answer to a question that I was chewing on last week pops into my brain. I call it ‘Creative Thinking Time.”

So, each day now, when the day’s mine work is done, I set out with the blue dog at my heels and a few of his treats in my pocket. There’s a trail heading away from the mine village that runs up to a gap between two big broken hills. A creek runs through this gap and, in the middle of the gap is a waterhole. After big rains it’s a good place to swim. Now it’s barely a puddle, filled with dead looking water.

This slowly dwindling water still brings life. Kangaroos drift in for a late afternoon drink, a lizard suns itself on the rocks, insects buzz and small bright birds flit through from the surrounding scrub. Blue Dog loves this place full of scents of many animals. Me, I mostly sit on a flat rock and gaze out over the water until the sun tells me it’s time to head home, shower and ready myself for dinner.

A fortnight has passed since Blue's advice, and I'm yet to receive any great inspiration, though stray ideas flit through my head like the birds over water. I kick at the dirt beneath my feet, feeling mildly frustrated, wanting a great idea to come. My foot hits an obstacle, a small roundish rock half buried in the soil. Absently, I kick away more soil until a rounded shape emerges.

The object has a smooth regular curve and tapers to a flat edge at the other end. I reach down and pick it up, pushing the loose dirt aside. It rests in my hand, smooth and heavy. I look closely, noticing a pattern of grind marks where this thing was shaped. Bits of black resin appear to have attached it to something. A slow realisation dawns; this is the head of a stone axe, one fashioned by a dark-skinned man, perhaps hundreds or even thousands of years ago.

I'm utterly fascinated. The shape and balance are perfect. Though some may see it as a crude tool, I see it as a talisman of a forgotten age, buried by layers of dirt and time. I want to know more about the ancient lineage of people who lived in this place back then.

My childhood schooling has been rudimentary. Between working to help support myself and my mother, skipping school because the maths and physics were beyond me, and getting into fights and having to keep away from other kids who said bad things about our family, I probably missed a quarter of school days. On days I did go, my attention was often elsewhere. Sure, I know how to read and write, my basic counting is fine, and I'm able to follow drawings and instruction manuals for the machinery I've worked on, but that about hits the limit of my knowledge. I did quite like the English classes where we got to read a book and then talk about it. I also liked social studies where we learnt about other people across the world and their customs, from early to modern times, people with interesting names like Egyptians, Aztecs and Incas.

Of aboriginal history, I know almost nothing, and as little about the white settlers to this land, though I know they killed and drove out many black people; that was one story my mother had clear in her mind.

Come to think of it, I've never really concerned myself with my own history, who my mother and father were, where they came from, what they did before. I vaguely know I have an aunt, my mother's older sister, as we got a letter from her once, but if I've ever met her I don't recall it. She never came to the funeral. Perhaps she never knew. I think my mother said she lived in a flash house in Queensland, though I'm far from sure that's right.

Thinking of my family gets me wondering about my mother's and my heritage. While I readily pass for a white fella in truth my skin is a quarter shade darker, almost a bit Middle Eastern in colour. Some people used to say my mother and I had a dash of the tar. I guess they meant a bit of blackfella. It was never said in a nice way, but as one amongst many insults, I never paid it much mind.

We never hung out with black kids in their camp down by the creek, but my mother always treated the odd strays from this camp kindly, particularly ones who came to our house looking for a bit of food. So, maybe, there's a grain of truth in the dash of blackfella, who knows? The idea there's that lineage in me is exciting.

These thoughts wash through my head like a whirlpool, spinning in expanding circles. But slowly they coalesce into a clear plan. I know what I want to do. I want to find out about the people who once lived here before the white men came, the ones who made this axe head I've just found.

It's an idea that excites me. I doubt it will make me rich, but it's what I really want to do.

I look at the piece of stone in my hand and wonder what to do with it. It feels like it belongs here; it's not mine to take. I can't just drop it on the ground where I found it. Then someone else will see it, pick it up and take it away.

I know enough about these things to know it's valuable and others up here make money by finding and selling these things. I must hide it.

I look around for a good place and soon find it, a crevice between two rocks in the creek bank that forms a mini cave, just big enough to put my hand inside. I rest the stone in the bottom of this space and walk home, my head afire and buzzing with excitement.

That night, I ring Patsy, my first call since she left, and I tell her of my plan. She sounds genuinely delighted to hear my voice, and I feel a glow of affection for her as we talk. I tell her of my plan, happy to be able to release my enthusiasm.

She responds with equal enthusiasm. "The place to begin is the library," she suggests. "I know the librarian, Jenny. I'm sure she'll help you."

We chat for a while before she says, "I've missed you, and I have space for you to come and stay. Get yourself on a flight and visit me this Easter."

She's right. I need to get out more, and I've never been to Perth, at least outside its airport. The thought of days and nights spent with her gives me a pulse of excitement, so I promise I'll visit.

The next day, I leave work slightly early and visit the library in the town centre. It's near closing time, so I won't be able to stay long, but I'll be able to introduce myself to the librarian and drop Patsy's name.

Jenny is as friendly and helpful as Patsy said she'd be. She shows me how to search the shelves. I leave, half an hour after closing time, with three books and lots of other ideas. She tells me to come back anytime, and if I need after-hours access, she'll arrange a key.

That night, I stay up until almost midnight reading, jumping from book to book as the history engulfs me, layer after layer and story after story. I can feel my mind swelling and expanding with all these new facts.

I return to the library most days after that. My study is pretty random at first, but I gradually I get the idea of keywords and indexes and begin to understand the way the library catalogue works and how it can help me.

A fortnight later, I'm on the plane to Perth for Easter and a week away. Seeing Patsy is like a homecoming and, at first, we barely talk as we devour each other's bodies. With our lust eventually satiated, we begin to talk.

She says, "I've missed you so much Jim. I do love being here and studying, learning so much new, but my life feels like its missing a part without you. It's not just the sex, great though that it, it's talking over ideas with you.

I say, "I've missed you too, it is partly learning from you and part being able to talk about anything and everything with you. You've made my world a much bigger place."

She continues, "I'm so glad you've found something else you want to do, to learn and study. You may not have done much school, but you have an amazing mind, and a great ability to learn and discover new things.

So for two days we alternate between intense talk and mind-blowing sex. Then we spend another two days touring and exploring all parts of the city.

The final day before I return, she tells me she has someone she wants me to meet. "She's called Madeline, and she's a senior lecturer in the History and Archaeology Department. She specialises in aboriginal history and archaeology. I've arranged an appointment for you."

Madeline is lovely and enthused with my plan to study aboriginal history. "If you'd like, I'll put your name forward for part time enrolment in some courses as a mature aged student. You'd have to come to Perth, twice yearly, for on-campus courses, but the rest of the study can be done by mail, just the same as Patsy did."

I weigh up the idea of becoming a student. It seems very far removed from my upbringing and lack of formal education, but I can see it's a path to a different future. And the combination of Madeline and Patsy's enthusiasm is infectious and persuasive.

In the end, I agree to enrol and to do my best. For the first term, I'll limit myself to one subject, 'An Introduction to Aboriginal History'.

If that works out, I may upgrade to two subjects a semester after that. The idea of getting a degree seems impossibly far away, but my priority is to learn things, not to get a piece of paper.

Chapter 11 – Jim – Iron Mountains

Life goes on at Tom Price. I have a regular job driving a dump truck, which carries a vast weight of ore blasted from this iron mountain. I'm very well paid for my skill, which is modest but efficient. Blue and I remain close friends, though we're both busy and can't meet up as much as we used to.

But what really drives me is my interest in the world that surrounds me, this place of iron mountains. They comprise layer after layer of iron rich rock. It was laid down under the sea a supposed two and a half billion years ago. This seems an impossibly long time in the past, but there's no arguing with the bands of iron I see every day, which are six hundred metres thick and grade at up to sixty percent iron. When I do rough numbers in my head, with steel selling at around fifty dollars a ton, what's in the back of my two-hundred-ton dump truck rapidly adds up to a lot of money. No wonder they built a town here to mine this stuff.

Tom Price is the highest town in the west of this huge land. It sits at almost two and a half thousand feet above the sea, amidst a vast surrounding weathered sand plain, which runs west to the ocean and east for thousands of miles across Australia's great deserts.

It's said these mountains were once ten thousand feet higher, but that the relentless work of wind and rain has slowly eaten them away, grain by grain, until what now remains are their relics, things like the hard fossils of dinosaurs buried in mud and sand, telling of how these huge creatures once roamed the land. In the case of these mountains, it's the tale of how a huge mountain once towered over this land and has slowly shrunken into the desert, though still enough remains to tell its story and, at the same time, it has become a huge store of wealth for the cities of our planet. It gives us the steel that powers the buildings of our modern civilisation.

Buried within the cracks and crannies of this ancient mountain range are remnants of human and animal lives of the past, such as the aboriginal stone axe I found.

Now I have an all-terrain car, I can explore these places. My explorations take me to the places where ancient rivers have carved their way through these ranges. Permanent waterholes sit alongside banded rocks where water has cut through hard iron layers. It was these rich places in a barren landscape where the first peoples mostly lived and, as I travel ever further afield, I can see their traces, more stone tools, old camp sites and pictures on rock faces. Exploring and learning more about this is a new passion that consumes me.

Jenny at the library becomes my de facto research assistant then, as my interest lights her thirst for knowledge, she comes with me into the field. Before long she shares my bed at night under the stars. Like Blue, she once had a life in Perth before a failed marriage drove her north. As her children were almost grown and independent when she found her husband shagging his secretary, she packed her bags, left the marital home and moved far away. She sees her kids occasionally, but they're busy building their own lives.

As an avid reader with a hunger for knowledge, it wasn't long before she found herself in the job of librarian in this little, out of the way, town. She's twenty years my senior, and neither of us kids ourselves that this is a relationship with a forever future, but it suits us both well and adds its own pleasure to each night at the end of a days of exploration out in the baking sun.

Jenny has also found an unused room at the back of the library where we can research and catalogue our finds. It's soon full of boxes and trays, some of which get packaged up and sent off to Perth for further analysis; others just sit there in their numbered spaces, a documented record of our trips and findings.

Jenny has enrolled in her own course, a subject far more complex than mine; she's doing a PhD on the earliest life forms found in these rocks and sediments, creatures dating back to the Proterozoic era, the time when it's thought living things were only just beginning.

I'm now well into my second term and studying subjects in Archaeology and Aboriginal Anthropology. It's basic stuff, but it helps me understand what Jenny and I are finding. More importantly it feeds my interest in newly discovered fields of knowledge. I doubt I'll get a degree, but that's not important. All I really want is an understanding; something to give a frame of reference into which I can place my discoveries. I also want to know more about the first peoples of this land, though this is just a half-formed thought.

My discoveries in the company of Jenny fill up my days and nights in an interesting and pleasurable way that allows me to drift along with no real thought of what my future may hold. Before I know it, over three years of living at Tom Price have rolled by, and I've achieved an overall understanding of my field of study.

During that time, Blue has become a budding entrepreneur. He was a qualified motor mechanic in Perth before his family life fell apart, so he'd naturally gravitated to working in the machinery shed up here. Over the last three years though, he's developed an interest in explosives and moved into a job of setting up the charges to blow apart the sides of mountains.

He first began doing this work at the Newman mine, but as he's become ever more highly skilled, he started selling his services at various mines around the Pilbara locality. It's been a lucrative business for him so far.

In the third year of him doing this, he asks me to join his enterprise, not because I've any skill in the field, but he likes the idea of a business partner. "I know you value your studies, Jim, but you'll never make any real money from it. If you join me in business, you'll secure yourself a great future income. Just have a think about it."

I take him up on his offer and find time to learn what he can teach me. He offers me a 20% shareholder stake, which seems excessive for what I can offer him in terms of skill, but there's nothing like owning a part of something to make you work hard to grow it.

Now, when we meet, he teaches me the basics of explosives and their use, although this is not what he needs me to do. Blue is sharp as a tack, but his own academic history is limited. What he needs is somebody he trusts to help set up the business side of things and, as my studies have made me literate in fields of calculation and writing up quotes, that becomes my role.

He says, "In my experience, outsiders rob you blind when you're not looking. I'll never have to worry about that with you in charge of that part of the business."

All in all, it seems to work well. I keep track of the costs and all things money, and he makes sure the explosive work is done well.

In the fourth year, he goes out on his own. He prospers as the work floods in. I stay with my job at Tom Price, and we do most business over the phone at night. I know, at some point, I'll have to decide whether to throw in my regular job and work full-time with him.

In the meantime, I keep on with my other work and studies and my bush trips. Some of my favourite places have become the likes of Hamersley Gorge and the Fortescue River, places where water has carved incredible shapes down through endlessly layered rock.

In the summers, when rain is abundant, these places come to life with incredible richness, and I find I'm equally interested in gazing over the landscape vistas of layered rocks and in seeking out the ancient stories they tell of an earlier land that was here a millennia ago.

It's hard to get much information about this place's early peoples, those first aboriginal inhabitants. There's clear evidence they were here and used this place, but it seems many of their stories are lost in the same way as my own history has been. Knowing this makes me want to seek out my own family story too, but I never quite get around to it.

Chapter 12 – Jim – The Rock Fall

Things that change lives often come from nowhere.

I'm eating my lunch one day when I hear on the ABC news that there's been a rock collapse at Newman Mine, and a worker has been killed. I don't give it much thought at the time, as the story on the local ABC radio is over in seconds. I must ring Blue when I've finished work that afternoon to get the inside story. He'll surely know what's happened.

As I end my shift, more news has filtered through. The miner was setting charges on the rock face and had been caught beneath a boulder that came loose and crashed down onto him. He died instantly. An hour later, the dead man's name is released. It's Blue.

My boss gives me immediate leave, and I drive to Newman that night. Mine workers always stand solid in the face of tragedy.

Before I head off to drive there, I volunteer to ring Blue's ex-wife and children to pass on the news, as I've met them all a couple of times.

Evie has been Blue's steady partner for a long time now. She shares a house with him and works as his bookkeeper. I've often talked to her about the accounts, getting quotes and other parts of this business. With Blue's business success, they'd put on hold the idea of buying and living on a farm.

Evie is totally shaken when I arrive, unable to make sense of what's happened. "I'm three months pregnant. We were planning on announcing our wedding next month. Blue wanted you to be his best man."

Her words hit me hard. The happiness of the family they would have been is gone.

"They told me he was barely recognisable when they pulled him out," she said. "His clothes and hair were the only way they were able to know for certain it was him."

We chat for the rest of the night as we start to come to terms with what's happened. The arrangements over the next week proceed in a quiet blur: flights for relatives, plans for a funeral in the town with all his friends gathered, the sorting out of the affairs of the business.

Blue has now employed an extra worker trained in explosives. He is keen to buy out the business in full, so we agree on a price to be paid in instalments over the following two years as it generates cash.

I want all the proceeds from the sale to go to Evie, but she insists she only take Blue's 80% share and that the other 20% is mine. Her own share, plus her savings with Blue, means she can go ahead and buy the farm they'd planned to get in the future. "Blue would have liked me to raise our child there. It was our dream."

The funeral is a big affair. Most mine workers and families from Newman come along and many drive in from other places such as Port Hedland, Karratha and Tom Price. There is also a bevy of friends from Blue's days in Perth, who've flown up. Several of Blue's mates speak, telling stories of the man he was. His ex-wife and children say their own words. Neither Evie nor I speak. Her grief is too raw, and any words seem too little for me.

Evie wants to be gone as soon as the wake is done. It is too painful for her to stay at Newman with all the memories of her life with Blue.

A month later I wave her goodbye as she boards a plane. Then it's me alone with odd memories and remnants of my best mate, a man who had been like a father, older brother and friend all rolled into one.

Chapter 13 – Jim – Return

With Blue gone, I lose my mojo. I can't find the energy or desire to study or go out bush. I drop out of my university course and work the minimum hours required at the mine.

Jennifer has morphed from a lover into a friend over the last couple years. She now has a steady man in her life. There are plenty of other women in town who I sometimes spent intimate time with, but I can barely be bothered with that either. One night stands with women, who are barely my friends when I wake up the next day, all seem meaningless.

Jennifer finally pulls me up short one day, after I've spent another late night at the pub, looking badly dishevelled.

She pushes herself into my face. "You need to get a grip on yourself. You're too smart to become the town drunk. You need to find yourself a new life."

The next day she turns up at my door with a one-way airline ticket to Sydney. "It's time for you to go back and see if you can find any trace of your wife and daughter. You'll never move on until you do. Do if for me and do it for Blue. Neither of us wants to see you wasting your life."

"You know I can't just take off from work like that, with no good reason."

"I've already talked to your boss. He wants you to sort yourself out as much as me. He's arranged for you to take a month's leave for a trip back to Sydney. After that, if you want to come back to your job, you can. It'll be up to you to buy the return airfare."

So that's that. The final night my work mates put on a farewell in the pub. Lots of townsfolk I've known over the years come along, all wishing me well, some saying there's a job back here if I want it. Others say they don't want to see me again until I know what I want to do in my life.

I appreciate the straight talking and promise them a postcard with the news.

It is strange to be standing back in Sydney after over five years away. A part of me feels I've barely left, but another part that I've lived a lifetime since then.

One of the first places I go to is the house where Cindy and I once lived. It is no longer a boarding house but has been bought up by somebody with money, now with a neatly trimmed garden and a new coat of paint. I watch a woman driving a Mercedes pull into the drive and let herself and two schoolchildren into the house. It is clear this is no longer a down at the heel neighbourhood.

That night I walk around the old haunts of Kings Cross I'd once known, but there are only strangers to be seen. There's still sharp rawness to my memories. When my night is done, I decide I won't come back here again.

I find a place to stay in Newtown, an unfamiliar part of town I barely know. The strange thing is that it feels like home in a way the country's west never has, almost as if I belong here.

My month away from work passes quickly, and I ring to say I'll be staying here. In that moment, I know I want to use what money I have, a tidy sum, to buy a home. It's time to have one real thing of my own.

The Sydney housing market has begun a big journey from cheap to expensive while I've been away. I could go out west around Blacktown and Penrith and buy something with change to spare, but the only Sydney I know is the part in close, the part where the old houses and history are located, as well as my memories of Cindy and Emily. So the beating heart of Sydney is where I search for my house.

My search takes three months. While, at first, I find nothing I can afford, it doesn't deter me. The right place will come along in its own right time. And time is a thing I have plenty of. I've learned how to spread it out using small events to put marker posts in its passage.

My belief that I'll find the right place at the right time eventually leads me to a small real estate agent on a side street near Redfern Station. There is no gaudy advertising to mark the place, only a small sign that proclaims: FOR THAT HOUSE WITH A DIFFERENCE, SEE US!

I tell the man at the counter what I seek and the limit of my funds. He scratches his head for a brief moment then a light bulb goes off in his eyes. "I may have just the thing. A woman brought the title in to me yesterday. She's selling the property of a relative who died some years ago. She found the title amongst some old papers she was sorting through. I haven't visited it yet. I don't think it's anything flash.

"I checked the Title Deed with the Land Titles Office yesterday afternoon, and it's all good. They found the original deposition on file from a time when it was converted from an old title dating back to God knows when, to a current Torrens title.

"Why don't you drive out with me to see it. There are no keys. I gather the door's boarded up to stop squatters, but I have a hammer and a few tools. Between the two of us, I reckon we should be able to get the door open and get inside to check it out.

"I think, if you put cash on the table, this lady is odds on to accept your offer. Most likely she'll take your instant dosh for a quick, easy settlement and count herself lucky.

If you like it enough, I'd put up 90% as a bargaining point to leave wiggle room. If you get it for what you have, you'll have struck a fine bargain."

I nod, "Sounds like a plan to me."

The house is as bad and ugly as the real estate agent suspects it might be, but I love it from the moment I see it. And I love it even more once I step inside, where the old flagstones and fireplaces tell me stories of people who've walked here and of those who've sat in chairs for fireside conversations. I hear the house's whispered voice calling out to me. "Come home, return to the place you belong."

I never check out the title and I never use a solicitor. I increase my offer price by half of my reserve ten percent following the agent's advice. With that the deal is done.

I pay over the cash, half of which has come from my share of Blue's business. I think he would have been proud to see me finally have something of my own.

It takes two weeks until all the dealing's done.

I move in and put my own lock on the open door.

Chapter 14 – Kate – New Family

I go home in a daze. Can it be true that I've found my biological father and a picture of my mother? She certainly looks like me, and the pendant around my neck looks a lot like the one in her photo though the detail is indistinct. What most convinces me is the certainly in Jim's eyes. I have a pretty good radar for bullshit. I can feel none here.

I'm amazed and tearfully grateful that I'm holding a picture of my mother in my hand. When I have my own copy it'll be something I treasure forever. Already, I can't bear the thought of ever losing it.

I'm excited to tell my mum and dad the news and show them the picture too. They've helped me search so many times and know the bitter taste of disappointment as well as I do. Having answers about my parents is the first step in closing a hole in all our lives, and they know their role in my life will never be replaced.

Half an hour later, I'm sitting at the kitchen table, the picture lying face down in front of me. "I've something to show you and Dad," I say to Mum. "Could you both come here and sit down?"

Dad straggles in from the garden, finished with his daily weeding ritual. He washes his dirty hands at the kitchen sink to the tut-tuts of Mum. "There's a laundry sink for that, dear." She pours us all a small glass of wine.

When they're both sitting, I turn over the photo. "Do you know who that is?"

Mum looks at the picture. "It's obvious, isn't it? It's a photo of you, but when was it taken I've no clue. You look about twenty. I don't think I've ever seen it before, or the clothes you're wearing. Whose is the little baby?"

Dad has always been the observant one. He looks at the photo closely. "Well, it's like you, but it's not you. Similar but different. A long-lost sister perhaps? Please give us a clue?"

"How about I tell you that I'm the baby."

Mum's hand flies to her mouth. "Oh my God, is that a picture of your mother?"

Dad looks equally stunned too as the penny drops. He raises wordless eyebrows, as if seeking answers from the heavens above.

My words have fled me too. All I can do is nod.

Finally, I manage, "I think so."

Bit by bit, I share the whole story, at least those little parts of it I know.

Dad, ever practical says, "Let's go meet Jim, shake his hand, say hello. He's part of our family now too!"

Mum vetoes the idea. "Perhaps tomorrow. I'm sure he and Kate have had a huge shock and have a lot to process today. It's big enough for Kate finding the parents she never knew. How about for him, finding a daughter who vanished more than thirty years ago when she was a bare month old."

Dad nods. "You're right. Then how about we ask him around to dinner tomorrow night, or maybe the night after, once Kate has had the chance to meet him again? Would you invite him, Kate?"

My family is so practical, and it's a relief that they've so readily welcomed the news about my other parents. Not that I'd expected otherwise, but still it's still a relief there's no sense of threat to our relationship. This is part of what I love about them. Not only is there unlimited space for me, but there's also plenty of inclusion room for others.

Before I leave I pull them in for a big group hug. "You know you'll always be Mum and Dad number one to me. Nothing will ever take that away."

Late in the afternoon, just as spring sunshine is falls behind the tall city buildings to the west, I decide not to wait until tomorrow to see Jim again. I've waited too long for this day already to want to wait any longer now.

I must buy him a gift and I'm not sure what to buy at first, but him telling me he loves flowers and of his plans to put a flower garden in at his house comes back to me, and so I buy a big bunch.

As I drive through the convoluted maze of back streets to his house, I hope he's in and hasn't gone to the pub. He did talk about having drinks with mates.

But no, his car is parked out front, and I can see him sitting, book in hand, in a plastic chair out the back in the late afternoon sun. I knock on the door.

He welcomes me and brings me around to the back. "This is a welcome surprise. I didn't think I'd see you again until tomorrow."

I hand him the flowers. "I hope you like these."

He gives me a craggy grin. "But of course. You've picked ones that were my mother's favourites. They grew in her backyard and, even when she got sick, she loved to sit amongst them. I'd put a few in a vase next to her bed each night. They always made her smile."

I may be mistaken, but I'm sure I glimpse the trace of a tear in his eye as he speaks of her.

"She must be my grandmother. Would you tell me more about her, please?"

We sit and talk, and talk, and then we talk some more. All the light has gone apart from a faded glowing reflection in a window, but neither of us ready to stop talking and sharing details of our lives, so the words continue to flow.

Finally, he sees the cold of the settling night is making me shiver. "You'd better come inside for a cup of tea and piece of toast. I'd offer you better fare, but the pantry is a bit bare."

As we walk in, I ask what I should call him.

His grin is infectious and, in it, I see glimpses of my own. "Well, my birth name was James, and that's the formal name I still go by. Everyone else calls me Jim. That works for me if it sits comfortably with you."

We sit inside and share tea and toast. It seems we have a shared passion for golden syrup on our toast, and we eat slice after slice until all the bread is gone. It's strange how family traits run on. These little things give me comfort in seeing glimpses of a family I never knew.

Finally, as time moves close to midnight, he says, "You should go. I'm sure you must have work tomorrow, as do I."

Before leaving, I pass on tomorrow's invitation for dinner. By the open door he offers his hand to shake. It seems too formal even though he's still a stranger, really. On impulse, I hug him. He's a few inches taller than me, still strong despite the creeping signs of age.

As I feel these arms go around me and feel the hardened power in his body, like my Dad's but different, it's as if a dam bursts deep inside me. Next thing I'm crying.

Like a father should, he enfolds his arms around me and holds and comforts me. It feels like coming home to the place I never knew, but that's always been there, waiting for me to find.

Chapter 15 – Mick – Back from the Future

I have been living in my new house for four years and business has been good. I have plans drawn to build a bigger and grander house out at Burwood next year, several miles along the road to Parramatta. But my base remains here, both for my brewery and my stone cutting business. I now have two acres of land on a long-term lease, and have submitted an application to convert a smaller part, the parcel where the house sits, to a freehold title. That way, the ownership of my house is separate from my stone business. The house itself has been finished for three years now, and it is a comfortable place to live. The heavy stone walls keep in cool in summer and warm, with the fire alight, in winter.

In its position back from the main road, the house offers me privacy for both my day business and for my secret brewing business. On busy days, I have a dozen workers cutting and finishing stone blocks brought from the quarry in rough form. I have built a steam engine, modelled from those of James Watt and George Stephenson, which greatly increases the power and speed of my stone cutting. It uses spinning discs of hard rock and forged steel to cut through and shape the soft sandstone, giving a smooth finish.

It is a good business and makes money, but it is really little more than a diversion from my main enterprise, which begins as the sun sets. I live in the main room of my house and have a separate eating and kitchen area in an outbuilding to make it clear to all workers that my house is my castle and visitors are unwelcome. The main room of my house is little more than a bedroom, with a door to what passes as a storeroom next door.

When the sun goes down, my storeroom and the hidden entrance to the place below the ground where I operate a still is opened. Down there, I produce a premium spirit in unmarked bottles on which my patrons then stick their own labels, just like the ones that accompany their imported spirits, on which they pay duty. My product sells for a small but useful discount from imports which makes it profitable for them and even more profitable for me. I also keep a few bottles aside for myself to enjoy at some later time which I have labelled with the name of Michael Kelly to bear witness to its Irish heritage but not identify me.

This cellar was dug with the help of my aboriginal friends after the main house was built. It has vent holes cut through the dirt, each covered by a heavy stone boulder, along with vents into the chimney in the main room above. These ensure the air down there remains fresh and healthy for my workers. The dirt from its excavation was taken and added to material at my stone works site, which didn't attract any attention as there was always a pile of refuse from the business in which to mix it. This was carted away with the other rubble to serve as fill for new building sites, places where raising or levelling the ground was needed before construction.

Four aboriginal ladies from the local camp work at night as my brewing workforce. I have taught them the art of brewing, and they follow recipes handed down through my family line but also use some local variants depending on what supplies we can source. The quality of my spirit is consistently good as it is never cut with cheap imports to make it go further. On this basis, many hoteliers prefer it. Not that they know the source. I sell only to four known distributor middlemen, and my business model is that I make, they sell, and we all profit.

Both their business success and personal safety rely on no details of our transactions ever getting out. One time a selling agent got careless with my privacy. By strange coincidence, three days later, his fly blown corpse was found by the water's edge in Cockle Bay. It served as a salutary warning to the others.

The aboriginal camp on my doorstep is a great asset. It gives me daily workers and keen observers who tell me if anyone undesirable is hanging around. It has also given me a bed companion, and she has birthed a brown-skinned baby in whom I recognise my features. It seems a fair trade that I support her and the rest of her tribe with work, food and money as needed. In return, they make my business prosper and keep it safe.

Some people say that, when I build my new fancy house, I must find a wife from the rich new settlers who arrive, someone to be mistress of the grand house. Perhaps, but as of now, I have no need of further female companions. The woman who birthed my son is a delight, and perhaps, in another year or two, she will give me another child.

Another year has passed, and still my business prospers. I now have the piece of paper granting me title to my house as separate from the lease on my other land. The document attests to it being a registration under the Registration of Deeds Act of 1825, and it lists a number for the title under a list called the Vendors Index.

Now I own the house on a separate parcel of land, I can, should I choose, sell off my stone building business and still keep the brewing business running, which is something I have half a mind to do.

I have a fit young Irish worker who reminds me of myself a decade ago. He wants his own start in life, and my building business, sold to him at a good price, could serve both his and my interests well.

His plan is to lease land down by the docks to run his business from. This makes sense and, if he does, I will gladly sell him my equipment and contacts for a modest fee.

After that, I will find another purpose for my block of leasehold land. As there is a good supply of water that I can pump with a steam engine, perhaps I will engage in an agricultural pursuit. My half formed plan is to grow vegetables, grains and malt and sell the excess in the town.

The town is ever creeping this way. It seems vacant land is in high demand for many purposes. I must ensure I keep my own domain private. It would never do to have any nearby neighbour to spy on my night activities. To make certain that does not happen, I must find a productive use of all the land that is mine.

Chapter 16 – Kate – My Long-Lost Mother

My life settles back into something like shocked order. I find myself continually glancing at the photo of my mother, as if intense looking can make her appear in my life like Jim did.

Work is busy, my days are full with heritage assessments to review and provide advice on, and with decisions to be made about what should and shouldn't be permitted under the NSW Heritage Act. This work has been my passion for almost a decade since I left university. I've grown good at finding the balance between the need for renewal or renovation and the imperative to retain our history in built form and keep it alive.

While this work is still my passion, it's lost its sharp focus. Of course, there's the matter of what to do about Jim's house, which is clearly highly significant and should be on the national estate. I'm especially curious about the stones he's found in his bedroom, which seem to indicate something lies below the floor. It needs excavation, but it has to be done professionally, so that all evidence is recorded and conserved. That costs serious money. I doubt it's reasonable to put this cost on him; it will leave him with nothing for his planned renovations, which are minor. I know how to do it myself, though it's many weeks of work, and I'm not sure how I'd fit it in around my ordinary job.

He could just relay his floor the way he found it and carry on with his reno work as planned, but that would be unsatisfying and potentially hide forever an important discovery. I probably want to know what's under there more than Jim does. More than any of that, though, I want to know about my real mother and where she's gone. Somebody will know the story of where she went.

I know Jim's given up looking for her, in truth because he believes she went off with another man, and the pain of that grew too sharp. He looks at it as a rejection of him as much as a loss of his wife.

I can't let go of the idea of finding Cindy. Jim's quite clear that Cindy loved me, and she wouldn't abandon me, yet that's exactly what happened. That's why there must be another person involved, one who knows what happened.

I have to find this person and hear their part of the story. Jim's also told me my mother would never have left me with a stranger. That narrows my search to someone she knew.

In continuing my search, I have to accept that she may have died back then, as if she was alive in the days that followed, she would have returned for me. But I'm clinging to the faint hope that she's still alive, and that there's an explanation for why she didn't come back.

I can't search for her alone. I need Jim's help. He knew many of her friends back then, so maybe he can help me locate them again now. He's my link to these people, even though decades have passed.

When I see him tonight, I'm going to put to him the idea of him helping me do this. I hope enough time has passed so he won't feel his pain so keenly, and he'll actually want to help me solve this puzzle of the past.

Jim agrees surprisingly easily. It's as if he knows his time for running away is over. Dredging his memory, he writes down every name he can remember of all those who knew Cindy. Most are only first names. The only one with a second name and address is Margaret, the older lady who helped him search. She was last known to live in Wollongong with her daughter, having moved there two years after Jim went west. He sent her a couple letters, and she sent him a couple of postcards, but despite his promises to visit her if he ever returned to Sydney, he never tried to find her again.

Even though she's probably in her 80s now, there's a fair chance she still lives at the address in Wollongong. So, the next Saturday, I drive us drive down to the coast to her address. We make good time and arrive around 11.00 am, a good time for a cuppa, or so Jim says.

Jim stands back a step as I knock at the door. He says I will appear less threatening to strangers and so be more likely to be welcomed.

A young woman, probably a few years younger than me, opens the door. "Hi. My name's Kate, and this is my dad, Jim. We were looking for an old friend of his. Margaret Bayley. Does she still live here?"

"Oh, you mean Gran. Her friends call her Meg. She's out the back hanging out clothes. I'll call her."

I wonder how she'll go recognising Jim over thirty years on, but her recognition is instant. "Jim, you old dog. Took you long enough to visit."

She turns to me, maybe recognising something familiar. "And you are?"

I like direct people, and she's certainly that. I laugh despite my serious demeanour. "Kate, though I think you last knew me as baby Emily. Jim's daughter. We've just found each other after all these years. You knew my mum, Cindy." I continue. "And we wondered if you could help us with finding her."

She looks at me closely. " Well, well, I do see the family resemblance. I'm so happy you've found each other again, but doubt I can help much. I did my best all those years ago, to no avail. What makes you think I can help more now?"

I look at her just as fiercely as she is looking at me, "Because somebody out there knows what happened to my mother and, unlike my dad, I'll keep looking until I find them and then her."

She steps back and smiles. "I like one with spunk. But I'm being rude. Come in for a cuppa and, while we drink, you can ask away."

After an hour we have five names. Using an old Sydney telephone book that she has in a cupboard, we also get three likely addresses, even if they're a decade out of date. The names are Susan Woods, a receptionist at a hotel who gave Cindy some cleaning work, Erica Miller who ran a flower shop next to the hotel, where appreciative customers often bought gifts for their regular girls at the nearby massage parlours, and Veronica Martin, a health care worker who helped a lot of the girls with any drug, alcohol or other health problems. The other two names are for a security guard at the hotel who kept an eye out for the girls, and the owner of a beauty and hair salon where they went for their hair and beauty treatments. The name we don't have, but I most want, is a woman who everyone called Lulu Lush. She was the owner of the brothel where Cindy once worked.

Margaret thinks her first name may have been Violet, but it's only a wild guess. The other name we really want to find is Cindy's best friend, Jo. Of course, Jo could have just been her working name and, as to a surname, we have no clues. Still, it's a great start.

We depart with many thanks and a promise to visit again soon, which I intend to keep even though I'm uncertain whether Jim will.

We decide to spend the afternoon visiting each of the addresses then, if there's time, visit Kings Cross as afternoon turns to evening and the brothel owners and their workers start to get out and about.

Erica Miller, the flower shop owner, is our first address in Bondi. We plan to say I'm trying to locate a friend of my mother's, somebody who worked in Kings Cross many years ago, and we thought maybe she'd remember her and even have some idea of where she had lived or gone after there.

An elderly man opens the door when I knock, and he listens to me. "You've come to the right address. My wife, Erica, ran the flower shop. I'm sorry to tell you you're too late. She passed almost ten years ago now."

"Would you still have any records of the business or her regular clients?"

"I never really knew too much about that or got involved. She sold it with all the records. Her client contact lists went to the new owners as part of the sale deal. I'm sorry I can't help you any more than that."

Our visit isn't a complete waste of time as, if we can find the new flower shop owners, it's possible they'll still have client names and addresses.

Our next visit is to a flat in Kensington to see if we can find the hotel receptionist, Susan Woods, but this time nobody answers.

"We should check the mailbox to see if she's still living here," Jim suggests.

The mailboxes are all in the lobby and are all locked. The slots are too narrow to slide my fingers through, but Jim solves our dilemma almost instantly by pulling out a bunch of skeleton keys. In seconds, the box is open. None of the unopened letters in it are addressed to Susan, so it seems we'll have to cross her name off the list as well.

Our third address is an apartment in an old multi-storey block in Potts Point. As we walk up to steps to approach the front door of this apartment, the door alongside it opens, and an older woman walks out.

Quick as a flash, Jim calls out, "Excuse me, we're looking for Veronica Martin. You wouldn't know if she's around, by any chance?"

The lady smiles in a friendly way and says, "I suspect she'll be shopping right now. She usually does that on a Saturday afternoon. She's normally back between five and six, just in time to make dinner for her husband. He should be home, but he's not great on walking to get to the door, so it's probably best to wait until Veronica comes back.

We return at five thirty, just in time to see a woman struggling up the stairs with shopping bags. Jim rushes forward. "Here, let me help you carry them."

'Thank you. That's very kind of you."

We follow her to the front door, and Jim places the bags down. She goes to thank him again, but I quickly cut in. "Actually, Mrs Martin, we're sorry to take up your time, but there's something we're hoping you can help us with."

She looks at me with an amused smile, "Oh, I see, there's always a catch to accepting the kindness of strangers. Well, spit it out. How can I help?"

She's clearly on the ball, so it seems dubious to try the fishing expedition approach on her. Instead, I cut to the chase. "Actually, my mother had a friend who ran a parlour in Macleay Street. Back then she was known as Lulu Lush. We wondered if you knew her, as we're trying to find her."

Veronica bursts out laughing. "Strange to say, but I do know her. I visit her now and then. She's in a nursing home in Elizabeth Bay. She's a good-hearted stick, though there's not much left up top now, if you know what I mean. That's the cruelty of dementia.

"She barely remembers me, so I doubt she'll remember your mother, but no harm in trying. It's probably a bit late to visit today, but if you go between three and five tomorrow, they should let you in."

We thank Veronica and head back to the street.

"She seemed strangely incurious about who we are," Jim says. "But, perhaps she has her hands full with other things."

By the time we've walked back into the street, we decide we've done enough for one day. "Mum's cooking a roast lamb for dinner and she wanted me to pass on an invitation for you to join us. Will you come around?"

We've grown comfortable in each other's company by now, and his reply is typical. "Roast lamb, did you say? Well, that sure beats scrambled eggs and baked beans on toast, which is what I have at my house."

At the house, I help Mum with final preparations, while Dad and Jim sit on the veranda sharing a beer. I hear my Dad say, "She's a treasure, isn't she, our Kate, or your Emily."

Jim tips up his beer and nods. "I like the name Kate. I'm well used to using it now. It suits her. I thank you for welcoming me into your family and for raising her so well. She's a credit to you both."

"You're just as much family now as she. It's a bonus for us all to have found you. I'm glad for us and for Kate that you are here. We couldn't have a child of our own, and so, when she came along, we felt so blessed. Now we feel doubly blessed that she has you as well."

It's hard to describe the sense of goodness that washes over me with hearing these simple words. He's right; I am doubly blessed to have two fathers. Now all I need to complete the circle is to find my other mother.

Chapter 17 – Mick – Way Back When

It felt like my life was starting to get to a good place.

I sold off the stone business last year, to my young Irish worker, for a tidy profit. Robbie, one of those naturally gifted stone masons, moved the business back to the docks at the other side of Cockle Bay. He has since added a stone quarry, so his raw material comes out of the ground next to his processing yard. There he has built an improved version of my original steam engine, which drives the wheels that do the cutting and shaping of the blocks. This is far more efficient than the manual cutting I was taught. When the blocks are ready to go, the boats come right alongside his yards and take them. That way he moves the heavy ones in big batches, and needs far less labour to do it.

Much building is now underway in Maitland, up on the Hunter River. It has become the colony's new settlement due to its river access and the fertile farmlands which surround it. The settlers and merchants of Maitland desire fine houses. They buy Sydney's best sandstone and take it there to build.

Robbie and I remain firm friends. I sometimes help him with big jobs when manpower is short. I still have skill enough, although my practice is limited these days.

My main focus now is on my own lands and my night brewing business. To this I have added a legitimate daytime brewing business, which produces small volumes of inferior liquor on which I pay the taxman customs duty.

I market this produce under an Irish Brothers Label. It is acceptable to drink but not memorable. Importantly it gives me a legitimate identity in this trade that is not directly linked to my own name. It makes little money, but serves as a good cover for my night brewing business, from which my real earnings come.

I only sell my premium liquor to good clients I trust, and I'm confident both they and I benefit enough from these sales to not broadcast the source. Most payment comes in gold coins, of which I have a steadily accumulating pile.

Alongside this business, I have ten acres of leasehold land where I grow fresh fruit and vegetables for the Sydney market. It also produces legitimate ingredients for my brewing business.

While the soil here is poor, being mostly sand, it drains well and is easy to improve with garden and animal waste. Most importantly, I have abundant water from my well. My steam engine now drives a pump to water my crops and, best of all, I have ready and willing labour force in the nearby blacks' camp, who do the hard work in the hot sun: endless hours of planting, weeding, watering and picking. There is even a reliable old man who drives the bullock dray, taking a stream of produce up town to the central Sydney markets.

Part of the land I lease is the land of the blacks' camp. It is good to own this place as it gives me control over who else comes here and lets me give these people protection from others of a less noble bent, those who would exploit their trust. I try to feed and care for them well, the way I would have liked to have been cared for when I was the servant of another while locked away in prison. They reward and respect me greatly in return.

I now have a black wife too, though I would not call her that out loud. She has given me a fine boy and two girls, the youngest who mostly runs around with her thumb in her mouth. They have tribal names, but I have given them names from my heritage as well. The boy is Connor, the name of my brother, and the girls are Maria and Angela, named after my aunts. My wife calls herself Yura Warawee. I gather Yura is like a tribal name, and Warawee is like a Christian name, but their customs are different, so it is hard to compare.

My wife is the real boss of our house and of her own tribe, a role she has taken since her uncle, who was Bennelong's cousin, has died. I like that she runs both our household and lands, leaving me free to travel to other parts of the colony to seek new business opportunities, and most particularly, to enjoy simple pleasures, such as sitting in the warm sun watching the birds flit through the trees while my children play at my feet.

It is only a pity I cannot marry her properly, done in a church in the way other folks do. That way she could come with me on my travels and to the homes of others in high society. But that just will not do. It is hard enough for me as a former convict to mix in upper society. For her it's impossible on account of her black skin. Some things are too big to change, so I must accept them.

All my life would be well, but yesterday a boat came. With the boat came a letter. The letter was addressed to me.

I have got few letters in my life. Neither my mother nor father can read and write. The local priest back home taught me a little when I served as an altar boy over a decade back, but I only fully learned this art since coming to the colony. Now I try to write a letter once a year to my family in Ireland, though I rarely get a reply.

The last one was three years ago, again written by the priest. Its main news was that my older brother, Connor, had died of pleurisy the winter before, and my younger sister, Marie, had married a fine man with fields ten miles away, so they saw her little. It only left my younger brother, Neil, who was about ten when they transported me, still living at home with my mother and father in their advancing years.

They have a small holding in the hill lands of West Cork. When I was a child, it produced little, just enough to feed us. We had a cow for milk, a few sheep and some stony fields, where we grew potatoes and other vegetables. At odd times, we bought a suckling pig in the markets which we fattened on a mix of old milk and inferior potatoes.

I sit and read this letter, which my father got the local priest to write. It has been very long in its journey to get here. I do not know how old my mother and father are, something above fifty each. They married young, and I am now thirty as best I can guess, and my youngest brother, is around twenty-three.

In the letter, I read about Neil taking over the working of the farm, though father still helps. He has made many improvements, having picked up much loose stone to make ditches, and he has started on building a second house for himself. He has bought a second cow and some more sheep, and even a horse to pull a cart which takes the extra produce to the village to sell.

All was going well until two months before this letter was written and sent.

One day, as Neil was driving the cart to town, the horse startled and reared, overturning the cart, which landed on top of Neil and broke his back. Now Neil is unable to walk. He sits at home propped up in a chair, and my mother minds him while my father struggles on trying to work the land. But my father's labours are not enough, and my mother is getting old and tired. Her health is poor with caring for my brother. My father now begs for my return, that I come home to help him. He thinks neither my mother or brother are long for his world and wishes for me to see them one last time.

I do not want to go, but think I must. It has been near on thirteen years since I was sent away. I wish to see them again, particularly my mother before she dies. It would give her comfort and I can only hope I am not too late. A boat sails for England next week. I know I must be on it.

It tears at my heart to leave my new family behind.

Chapter 18 – Kate – Marks in the Stone

This afternoon, Jim and I plan to visit the nursing home where Lulu Lush resides. I'm hopeful she'll reveal a path into my mother's past. The official visiting time is 3.00 pm.

I woke up this morning with a niggling curiosity about something, but I couldn't quite work out what was bothering me. It was frustrating the hell out of me not being able to put my finger on it and, in the end, after my mum told me she was sick of me wandering around the house like a bear with a sore head, I decided to visit Jim. We could at least talk about how we'd approach Lulu this afternoon.

As I park in front of his house, what's been bothering me comes like a lightning bolt. It's what first brought me to this house, the thing Jim and I've named 'The Buried Treasure' in an in-joke sort of way. Unlike trying to find out what happened to my mother, this is a mystery that I *can* solve.

I knock on the door. I push my way inside when Jim doesn't immediately answer, such is our familial familiarity.

"Jim, we have to get on and find out what's under the stones on your bedroom floor. We've been too distracted. Shall we have another look right now?"

He gives me a quizzical look as if to say, 'like mother, like daughter, always a new crazy scheme', but I can feel he's caught my enthusiasm too.

Typically practical he says, "Okay, what equipment do we need, and how do we do it?"

"Let me have a close look and document what's here. Have you got a good camera, you know, one with a flash and a proper close-up lens?"

"I suppose."

He goes and finds an old digital SLR, a Nikon, no less. It's a bit of a dinosaur, but it has a flash and a close-up macro lens, which is ideal for what I want. He even has a fresh set of batteries for the flash, and a new memory card.

I grin. "Welcome to your most important role as my research assistant. The pay is nothing except the pleasure of my company and, of course, a share of any discovery. I'll put your name, as co-author on any paper I write, a sort of father and daughter thing.

He says nothing in reply but gives me his own crooked grin. I know he's as keen as I am. We go to the bedroom and look again at the floor. It seems a lifetime since I first saw it. It's actually less than a month, but it feels as if an eternity has elapsed since that day.

Back then I was looking at a small mark on a stone a few inches from the base of the wall, rather than at the blocks on the floor, which are all plain. I knew from the moment I saw the mark it was a mason's mark.

Typically, early stonemasons in the colony took pride in their work and had a sense of ownership. Hence they often placed an unobtrusive but distinctive mark on a corner of a stone before it was laid, in part to stop others stealing their building materials.

I remember a research project another student did back when I was studying. She catalogued these marks and used them to date buildings based on their consistent use in a period. Some marks could be related to a specific builder, men whose names were in the early colonial records.

So I know this building has one such mark. It's most likely there'll be more marks on other stones here too, and I plan to find them. That's the first part of this research project: find as many marks as possible and record them all, Jim's job. Once I have this information, I'll dig out the PhD and compare my findings to those she previously recorded.

Half an hour of close looking finds five more identical marks to the one I saw on my first visit. They look a bit like a Celtic Harp, a thick curved line crossed by three fine straight lines. Each is about an inch in size and would be easily missed if not looked for. It makes me wonder if the mason was Irish, could this be a symbol of that heritage?

Jim catches my enthusiasm and carefully photographs each mark, taking pictures from a range of angles, both close up and from further away. He seems to intrinsically know what to do.

"Where did you learn your photography skills?"

"Oh, you know, here and there, out and about, part of my life in the West," he says cryptically.

As we work he tells me more. "I did something similar to this when I was working in the Pilbara, investigating signs of early aboriginal occupation and recording the findings. I'd met a woman who studied astronomy, and she encouraged me to take up that kind of study to educate myself.

"I never finished the degree, but I studied part-time for three years and learned lots of basic archaeology research skills." He smiles. "It's pretty remarkable to discover this parallel in our research interests and fields of study."

'It is pretty spooky. I'm planning on reading a PhD thesis about mason's marks. Someone, studying when I was, wrote it. Could be useful here."

He nods. "Well, if you find useful information from it, I wouldn't mind you making me a copy of the relevant parts for me to read."

"Consider it done."

Chapter 19 – Jim – The Cellar

Kate is amazing; she has such an eye for detail. Things I've seen but never understood jump out at her and tell her a story. Then, like a mad scientist, she documents everything she finds. It takes me back to my study days in the west where I learned similar things and was captivated by discovery in the way Kate is today. Today's bonus is that I'm now researching with Kate, who is both totally herself and a reminder of Cindy.

I love the way she's quickly become so familiar with me that she barges into my house and life without question, knocking is almost an afterthought.

Now we're fellow travellers on the same quests, searching side by side for answers to mysteries of the past. Having documented the mason's marks, we now need to find a way to lift the stones without damaging them. They only run for half the length of the room, so there'll be a way to get under the edge of one and lift it clear. We'll have a look where the stones end and the plain dirt begins.

We choose one corner of the room to test our theory, digging down a few inches below the level of the edge of the square cut stone. It's mortared hard against a layer of rough-cut stone below. Much thicker pieces can be seen running down deep into the earth likes sides of a subterranean structure. I wonder if an old well was dug here and later covered up with pavement stones before the house was built over the top.

We excavate half way across the floor and down about two feet. It looks like a buried wall runs across the room below the floor. It seems to run the full width of the room and disappears into the depths below.

It's curious and fascinating. It seems the square cut stones were placed sometime after the wall was built. They're laid tightly together without any spaces between them for mortar. Mortar only lies below, between them and the deeper stones, to bind them in place.

"We should stop now," Kate says as she's surveys what we've found. "From here on in it's a job for a team of professionals. The excavation needs to be done very carefully, under an excavation permit. Everything has to be fully documented."

I know she's right; we should stop now and let her report this discovery for more careful examination. But I really want to know what lies below.

"Could we carefully scrape out the mortar from underneath one stone and have a look? Just to see if there's anything to see below?"

She shrugs and smiles. "How about I go out and make us a drink and sandwich. It's lunchtime, and we'll have to clean up soon to get ready to go and see Lulu.

"I can't help what you do when I'm out of the room. If you got your tools maybe you could make enough of a gap in the mortar below to try and lever the end stone up. If you can make a space to insert a lever, then maybe you can break the mortar loose and lift up this edge of the stone. If we're lucky, we can see if anything interesting lies underneath, but I'll, hand on my heart, be able to say I did nothing to disturb the evidence. You found one lose stone and lifted it."

It's good enough for me. I set to work and, in ten minutes, I have a gap an inch across and two inches deep that I can slide a tyre lever into. I wiggle the tyre lever in and give it a big jerk.

Nothing happens. I scrape out more mortar, get my lever another half an inch deeper into the gap, and throw all my force into the tyre lever with a big heave. I feel nothing but hear a tiny squeak of movement.

The rock has separated along its length by a tiny amount from the stone below, though I felt nothing. I give a second big jerk, and the top rock breaks it free, mortar adhering to its underside in some parts and in other parts the mortar is still bound to the stone below.

"Come and look," I call to Kate.

She stands beside me and we each take a corner and lift. Our stone is two feet across each way and about six inches thick. It's heavy but slides up, coming free of the other stones beside it with a grating noise.

Once it's upright, Kate holds it steady on its side while I find a torch to look below.

The first six inches of the stone's corner rests on the edge of a side wall, which descends at right angles to the wall we've dug down against, then there's a gap that starts part way across. At its far end, the stone rests on a heavy crosspiece of timber below it, which is now supporting its full weight. The intervening space is just vanishing darkness.

I focus the light into the empty hole. Our heads and shoulders crowd together as we peer into darkness. Torch light penetrates the gloom to reveal old stone stairs descending into what appears to be a cellar below.

The gap is too narrow to climb through. So all we can do for now is look, imagine where the steps might lead, and wonder what lies below.

Chapter 20 – Kate- Meeting Lulu

It's just gone past three when we arrive at Elizabeth Bay Nursing Home.

It was unbelievably hard to tear ourselves away from gazing down the stairs into darkness. Jim desperately wanted to lift a second stone and make a gap big enough to squeeze his body through, but I talked him into waiting so we can report our find and it can be properly investigated.

He agreed, but I can tell he thinks he has a proprietary right to explore his own property, and I can't say I wouldn't feel the same way in his position. Even though what the law says is clear, I'm pretty certain that tonight, when I'm gone, he'll explore anyway, but I can't find it in myself to object. I just can't be involved.

No matter how much I want to explore too, I can't break the law and be a party to this. It's more than my job's worth. I just can't bring myself to casually flout a law I expect others to uphold in my day-to-day work.

It's different for him though. I owe him the loyalty to not interfere before I report what's found here.

When we speak to the receptionist at the nursing home, we both realise we've no idea what Lulu's real name is or anything about her that will help us identify her. Jim only met her the once, over thirty years ago, when he went with Cindy to say she was leaving. All he can remember is her dyed bright red hair, and that she had a pleasant face that once was pretty in her youth.

The woman at reception is probably hoping we'll leave, as we have no name. "I don't know any of the residents," she explains. "I only cover the admin and the visitor's book. I'm sorry I can't help you more. But without a name and room number, I can't let you in."

We're almost ready to give up and leave when a carer comes out with a patient whose family are waiting to take the person out for a visit. After she passes over her charge, Jim catches her attention. "I don't suppose you know a resident who sometimes calls herself Lulu?"

"Not many people call her that anymore, just a couple of women who once worked for her and still visit. Her name's Violet Montgomery. If you sign the book, I'll take you to her room. She likes visitors but doesn't get many anymore. She'll be happy to see you even if she doesn't know who you are. Sadly she's forgotten more than she remembers these days."

Jim shares a concerned look with me at these words.

We follow the carer down a long corridor that opens out to a room with a bright sunny view over a garden. We stop outside a door that leads off this area, and she gives a quick knock at the door and says cheerily, "Two lovely visitors for you, Violet. Isn't that a nice surprise?"

Sitting in a chair, looking out to the garden, is a smallish woman with faded hair somewhere between dark blond and grey. It looks like somebody comes to colour it occasionally, but it's not been done for a while.

Violet looks around with a start as we fully enter the room. Her eyes brush past Jim and the carer and lock onto me. "My God, Cindy, where have you been?"

It's the strangest thing to be mistaken for a mother you've never met, even if I bear more than a passing resemblance. Part of me is shocked to be mistaken, but alongside this comes a wild surge of hope. Violet is the second person I've met who knew Cindy. She must have known her well to remember her after all these years, when all else is a muddle to her. Perhaps she knew her better than Jim did and will have better insights into where she went. When Jim went looking for Cindy, when she vanished, he talked to her best friend Jo. When Jo couldn't give him any information, he didn't go to see Lulu, so I doubt he can help me in starting a conversation to get her to try and remember anything. It's all up to me.

I sit in the chair next to hers and take her hand in mine, hoping simple human contact may help her fractured mind find pathways to connect me to a past time with my mother. "I'm so glad you can remember Cindy," I say. "She was my mother. It'd be lovely to reminisce about her. Do you remember how she used to dress and wear her clothes?"

We begin a rambling half hour conversation of fragments. Cindy liked the colour blue. She wore her hair down when she was not at work but tied it up at work to make herself look elegant and keep it clean. Some of what Lulu says is hard for me to hear and probably harder for Jim, things about men who used to see her, the gifts they gave and the things they expected of her in return.

I'm determined to waste no chance to keep Violet's stream of memory flowing. Her words are more a jumble than real facts, but tiny gold nuggets are hidden amongst the dross. As her conversation subsides, I focus my questions. "Tell me about her friends, the other girls who worked for you? Do you know who supplied her with drugs?"

At the word drugs, Violet pulls back. "She was a good girl; she didn't like to do drugs."

I know from Jim that this is untrue, so I say, "Are you sure? Jim says she used meth and heroin?"

Violet's eyes glaze over for a moment then clear. They're a deep blue, almost purple, which fits her name.

It seems she's thinking, trying to connect things, but no words emerge. I focus my gaze on hers, willing her to remember. Still nothing.

I change tack, I ask, "How did you get the name Lulu rather than Violet? Violet is such a lovely name, and it suits your eyes."

Now something real is happening again. "It was Jo who first gave it to me," she says. "It seemed to fit, something about a movie star, or maybe a Broadway girl, you know in a stage show. I don't really remember that part now. But Jo said it was a great name for a Madam. I used to be Luscious Violet when I worked myself. Now, as the Madam, Jo said I needed a catchy name to draw the men. She suggested a few names, but the one that stuck was Lulu Lush.

"I felt it suited me, and I didn't want men knowing my proper name, you know. Some were real creeps. They would dig for information to use against you. A working name was much better."

After the last jumble, I feel another surge of hope. This must be the Jo who was Mum's friend. "Could you tell me about Jo? Was she one of your girls? Can you remember what she looked like, who her friends were?"

Violet is getting tired, and I fear I'm fast losing her; her eyes glaze over, and she looks away. I take her hand again and make a last effort. "Violet, can you remember Jo? Please try. I need to know!"

She shakes her head before finally saying, "You should know. She was your best friend. Why don't you ask her yourself, Cindy?" A tiny moment of lucidity follows. "She still visits sometimes. I have her card. She told me to ring her if I ever need anything."

She fumbles in her handbag sitting beside the chair. It's bulging with junk. Frustrated, she upends it onto the floor, where its contents scatter over a metre. She reaches forward, pushing things around this way and that, searching.

I kneel beside her. "Let me help you."

I start picking up the things, one by one, replacing them in the handbag after I show them each to her. Each time she rejects the item with a head shake and returns to the floor.

I keep going. Soon, I've picked up and returned most big items, and it's only the bits and pieces that remain, all still widely scattered. Violet has stopped her own searching and merely looks at each thing I show her, shaking her head. Soon there are only a dozen items remaining, mainly make-up, but also a few business cards and paper scraps. I collect all of the business cards and show them to her, one by one.

Suddenly, Violet's demeanour changes. She violently nods her head. "Yes, that's her. I knew I had Jo's card. That one is it. Such a sweet and lovely girl she was. Got a bit toffee nosed when she married a rich man, but she's always been good to me, and she still comes to see me when she can."

I look at the card: Josephine Flood, Design Consultant. Alongside this name is a small photo of a blond lady with attractive features. She looks to be in her fifties.

There's a Mosman address, phone number and web address on the card.

Jim looks at the picture and nods. "It's a long time ago, but I'm sure that's Cindy's friend, Jo."

Chapter 21 – Jim- What Lies Buried

I've returned home tonight strangely torn. Listening to Violet ramble on about my Cindy, it was almost like she was talking about another person, one who I never really knew. Some of the things she said about the men who hired Cindy felt like a knife through my heart, even after all these years.

Sure, I knew she'd survived by selling her body, but I treated that a minor part of her past life that ended when she met me. I realise now it was a huge part of her life for a long time before she met me.

I can't bear the idea we'll talk to Jo, and she'll say further things to tarnish my memory of Cindy, which I have held tight to for so many years. I've always feared she left me for another, a much richer man, but having a fear is not the same as really knowing. The idea of knowing terrifies me.

When we said goodbye to Violet, she first said a goodbye to Cindy, then wished us both well, and I felt a great sadness for how diminished she'd become.

Kate, on the other hand, was on an ecstatic high, bursting with enthusiasm at our big breakthrough. We'd found her mother's best friend. Now Kate wanted to follow up immediately and talk to her tonight.

I had to work hard to convince her to wait until tomorrow, arguing that its much better to see her in person at her office rather than ringing. Eventually she conceded, but with reluctance.

I really want another night with the memory of the Cindy I knew, not the one that Jo might tell me about.

It wouldn't surprise me if Kate rings her anyway. There's something of her mother's impetuousness in her character. I can't stop her seeing Jo, and I know how desperately she wants to know what happened to her mother, so I'll go with her tomorrow to Jo's work place and see if Jo remembers me. I'm hoping she doesn't, so I can just turn around and walk out. It's the coward's way, but sometimes seeing the past clearly is more terrifying than all other knowledge.

To take my mind off re-meeting Jo and what tomorrow might bring, I go to my bedroom and peer into the dark hole under the floor. I'm curious to know its secrets. My curiosity isn't strong enough to stop my mind from returning to Violet's remembrances of Cindy. Why was it so hard to hear about what men paid her to do? Perhaps because it was a closed book in our life together. From the first day, I trusted her and needed to know little of this past. Maybe I was wilfully blind, but it seems that suited us both. Did it make me naïve to who she really was? If I had the choice now, would I want to hear about her past from her?

These are unanswerable questions. In the end, this stalemate leads my attention back to the hole in the ground. At least here's a riddle I can solve.

I've given Kate my word I'll allow this to be done properly. But I don't want to wait until another day.

My impatience beats me. I get out my tools, including a bright light, which I focus on the hole. I kneel on my hands and knees and scrape away enough mortar to get under the next stone. I only need six inches more width, and I'll be able to slide my body through the gap.

I go slowly and carefully so as not to cause damage and get Kate into trouble. After half an hour of scraping and levering, I feel the second stone break loose from its bond. I lift it up and stand it alongside its mate.

Now the hole in the ground is well over two feet wide, and I'll comfortably be able to get my body through the gap. I move my portable electric light and mount it above the hole where its light can make its own way down.

Torch in hand, I wriggle my way through the gap and begin my descent.

The air smells dry and surprisingly fresh. I count my steps as I descend. There are fourteen before I reach the bottom. In front of me is a solid brick wall, but to my left is a heavy wooden door with an old-fashioned lock. The door is closed and locked. It's a tight-fitting door with no space around any of its edges to be able to get something through.

I look around for a hidey hole with a key. Whoever built this door is unlikely to have left the key too far away. It will be heavy and cumbersome to carry around, so I imagine they had a place to keep it out of sight but handy. I search around, but there are no loose bricks down here that could be slid in and out, and there's nothing obvious in the stairwell that could serve as a hiding place.

There is, however, a brick in the fireplace upstairs that lacks obvious mortar and moves slightly when touched. If I can slide it out, maybe there'll be a hiding place behind it.

I go up to the fireplace and check. The brick is still ever so slightly loose, as I remembered it. The space the brick slides into is tight, and no one would really notice the absence of mortar unless they looked very closely.

I use two screwdrivers, one on each side, to lever it out enough for my fingers to grasp the sides. As I grasp and pull the brick towards me, I expect a full-length brick like the others in the fireplace, but three quarters of the way out it comes free, and I'm left holding a brick with its end cut off. I look in the hole and see a lump of mortar to limit how far it slides in before its passage is blocked. Behind this loose mortar is an old and very tarnished iron key. It's of a size and shape that looks like it will fit the door.

I take it downstairs and fit it in the lock. The mechanism is very stiff from what feels like a hundred years of disuse, but with a spray of lubricant and some wiggling, it turns the lock, and the door swings open.

What I notice first is a sheen of glass, with my light faintly reflected. This light bounces back from hundreds of bottles stacked in rows and rows along one wall.

The room is perhaps ten steps long and four steps wide, an amazing sized space considering the small building that sits above it. The ceiling is made of heavy timber posts, all about six inches across, butted tight together except for a few places at both ends with gaps, perhaps air duct spaces. The stairs descend to the door which opens at one end of the basement. It seems that this room runs under the full length of the front room and perhaps half the length of the room from which the stairs descend.

At the far end, away from the rows of bottles, there is a complicated mechanism of tubes with a fire pit below from which a chimney runs up through the roof. I realise it will exit into the chimney in the fire place in my sitting room above and let the smoke out. When not in use, the chimney will let fresh air in, which must be why this basement room feels well ventilated.

It dawns on me this pipe apparatus must be an old still, and all the bottles must be its produce. It's impossible to say how old it must be. My best guess is it dates to sometime in the mid-eighteen hundreds.

At the opposite end of the room from the still is a wooden table and chair, along with two boxes, one of which looks like a valuable's chest. The other box is open and holds books, which look like old ledgers. Along the opposite side from the bottle store is a long bench which has a few tools and other implements on it, and also half a dozen empty bottles with labels stuck on them.

I pull out the ledgers. The name Mick Flynn is written on one. This seems to be his trading ledger with a running inventory of stock. There's also a slot to the side of the box, which appears to hold letters and other old correspondence.

It's too much to take in all at once, so I put the contents of the document box back in place and lift up the closed chest that sits alongside it. It's about a two feet long and two thirds as wide. It's amazingly heavy as if filled with lead. It has a lock, but this is not closed.

I flip the lid up. There are several cloth bags inside, perhaps eight or ten.

I pick one up and hear it chink. I undo the draw string and tip its contents into my palm. Gold glints in the distant light. It's a bag full of coins, golden in colour with some variation in size. My guess is that there are at least two-hundred coins in each bag and therefore well over a thousand all told. I don't know very much about the value of gold, then or now, but realise this is a huge treasure store. It may be worth more than all the rest of the house and contents combined.

I make the choice to close up the cellar the way I found it, but before I do I'll take the gold chest with me. Then I'll relay the stones in place.

Tomorrow, I'll be honest and tell Kate of my discovery, though maybe not about the gold. She's too straight and may want to declare it. If she does, the government will surely take it. I don't know much about the law, but this house is mine, as are all its contents. Taking this to its obvious conclusion it means this gold is mine, and I have no plans to give it to anyone.

In the end, the chest it too big to remove through the gap I've made in the paving stones, so I take out the contents and carry the bags to the back of my outhouse, where I put them in an old wooden toolbox. After that, I relay the stones. Tomorrow I'll buy mortar and relay them more securely.

Once the basement entrance is covered, I go into the backyard and dig a hole hard up against the back wall of the outhouse. The ground is dry and rocky, and the digging is hard, but, with patience, I work my way down until I have a hole a good three feet in depth and wider than the toolbox.

I rest the box in the bottom, wrapped in a sheet of canvas to keep it dry, then I refill the hole with soil, tamp it down until it reaches ground level, then walk around collecting old lumps of sandstone that litter my back yard. I pile these over the place of the burial hole until any evidence of it is hidden from sight. Now it looks like an old pile of rubble sitting against the outhouse wall. I'll leave the gold there until I have a better plan for its future.

When my work is done I look at my watch.

It feels like midnight, but it's only nine. Still time tonight to have a beer with my mates in the pub celebrating my find.

My shout of course, even if I can't say why.

Chapter 22 – Kate – Finding Josephine

I feel bad arguing with Jim as we walk away from Violet's nursing home. I have an overwhelming desire to ring Josephine immediately. It feels like I'm so near and yet so far from finding the truth. I'm really tired of endless waiting.

When Jim said he thought she knew something about what happened to my mother, I believed him. I'm even more certain now. It's as if every step is leading us towards her and with her is a path to the truth. I want to follow that path to where it leads without delay.

But at the same time, when I watched him absorb body blow after body blow, as Violet told us about my mother, all those true but muddled details of her life as a street girl, the men she served, the things she did, I feel my right is secondary to his.

He's lived with this pain for over thirty years. I can see, every time her name is said, that he's never stopped loving her, that she sits in a sacred place in his heart. So, despite my desire to contact Josephine tonight, I won't. Seeing her is something we must do together.

Instead, I'll go to work in the early morning and organise my day and week. I'll clear free time for our house search and book time off tomorrow afternoon so we can go to Mosman together to meet Josephine.

She will be there; I'm sure of it.

When I'm back home, I Google her web page. She says nothing about her past, other than that she started this Mosman business twenty years ago, and it seems to have done well. It seems her company does fashion and interior design jobs for the glitterati. Testimonials over the last decade along with many newspaper clips and other media grabs attest to this.

Office hours for new client visits are Monday from 2.00-5.00 pm, the same on Thursday, and 10.00-12 noon on Saturday.

I text a suggested time for tomorrow to Jim, and then go for a glass of wine with Mum and Dad, so I can tell them all the news. They're a calming source of common sense and agree with Jim's view that a face to face meeting is best.

With that my mind is calm. They're right. I've waited all this time. I know I can wait for one more day.

The morning passes with excruciating slowness as I organise my work.

Jim picks me up from outside work soon after lunch, and we crawl through the heavy city bound traffic along the Western Distributor and then over the Harbour Bridge before turning right into Military Road.

I know this part of Sydney well. I used to have a boyfriend in Neutral Bay, and Mum and Dad's house is five kilometres further north near Chatswood. We drive through the centre of Mosman until we come to a set of business apartments, of which Josephine's is one, just around the corner from the main street.

Now we're here, Jim is decisive and leads the way. I suspect he'll walk up to the counter and ask for her with no introductions or indication of what his business is. He's set his mind on what we're doing and nothing's going to stop him. I'll be watching her to see whether she recognises him or how she reacts.

The receptionist smiles as we enter and seems about to ask our business, but something about Jim's intense manner silences her. Instead she stands and discretely knocks on the closed office door behind her before entering and saying, "There is a gentleman to see you, Mrs Flood."

"What's his business?"

"He didn't say."

There's a brief pause before we hear, "Very well."

Josephine walks briskly into the reception area, a trace of a frown on her face. Halfway to the counter the penny drops. "Oh My God, Jim."

Then she looks at me and her hand goes to her mouth. "Cindy. No, of course you're not Cindy. Way too young. So, you must be Emily."

She puts her hands to her face and begins to cry, whether through happiness or pain I can't tell. It's as if some dam has broken, and her emotions are finally flooding out.

Chapter 23 – Jim – Josephine's Story

Josephine has brought us to the bar of a Mosman hotel and found us a quiet booth. She's composed again and says we're here so we have a quiet place to talk. Despite a veneer of composure, she seems even more shaken by this whole thing than I am. Kate's remarkably together as if she knew what Josephine's reaction would be and was ready for it.

Kate orders us drinks and settles us into our private spot with nobody near. She's straight to the point with Josephine. "I know you know something about what happened to my mother all those years ago, and that you couldn't tell Jim about it at the time. I realise you had your reasons. But I'm here to ask you to reconsider.

I've been looking for answers as to who I am and where I came from for over thirty years. If there was a way you could tell us what you couldn't tell Jim then you'd be helping me more than I can say."

Josephine is silent for many seconds, and we wait. It's as if she's collecting her thoughts and getting her mind into order. At last she looks directly at me and says, "This is something I wanted to tell you all those years ago. Not being honest with you then has tormented me ever since. But I made a solemn promise to Cindy that I wouldn't to tell you about it, not then, not ever, was how she worded it. She made me swear a promise on our friendship. So, despite all my reservations, I gave her my word."

She looks at Kate. "It feels like it all happened only yesterday, but look at you now. You're not that little baby any more. When I gave my promise to Cindy, it was to never tell Jim. It wasn't a promise not to tell you. If you choose to stay here and listen, that's a matter for you, Jim.

Or Kate could tell you later if you prefer to hear it from her."

It seems a fine distinction whether she tells Kate or me, but who am I to argue. Today it's time for me to finally know the truth. "Okay, I'll stay."

Josephine nods and turns to Kate. "A week after Jim crossed the mountains for work, Cindy turned up at my place early one morning with you in a pram.

"Lulu, who we worked for, had given me a private apartment out the back of the brothel. It was only one bedroom, a small place with a tiny sitting room and kitchen, but it had a private door that led to the street behind. That allowed me come and go as I chose without others knowing.

"She gave me the apartment in return for me doing other things like keeping an eye on the rest of the girls, managing the cleaning and tidying, and calling extra security if required. Only a handful of people knew where to find me, but Cindy was my best friend, so she was one of them.

"That morning when she turned up with you, you were only about six weeks old, but you were happy and smiling as usual, and we all sat outside in a little courtyard garden next to my place. It was an early spring day. Even though it had rained the birds were singing in the cherry trees in the yard and the bees were buzzing in the flowers. It seemed so peaceful and lovely. I could never have guessed I'd never see Cindy again."

She stops for a moment to compose herself again.

"As we began to talk, I could see Cindy was upset. She told me how much she loved you, Jim, as well as you, Kate. She so wanted to have a family with you, Jim, for you all to have your own place and have the things ordinary families had, like a house with a backyard, and toys and good clothes, plenty of food, money to go out to nice places.

"She said you'd been gone for eight days, Jim, and she'd thought she'd be fine minding Emily with you away. But it was much harder than she'd ever imagined, and she was worried about money as what you'd left was only just enough to pay rent and buy food if she used it carefully. That morning she'd broken your baby bottle, and then she burned the porridge she was cooking for breakfast. When she saw a rat in the house it totally freaked her out and was a kind of last straw.

"She knew they were only little things, but she couldn't afford to buy more bottles or other things for the baby or herself. She said when she was working for Lulu she'd always had plenty of money and could buy new clothes or other nice things whenever she wanted them. Worrying about money and having enough to feed and care for Emily was really getting her down.

"If I'd had your number, I'd have rung you, Jim, but I didn't know how to get in touch with you. She had the number of the farm you were working on, so she could ring you, but she only would if she really needed to. She didn't want to be a bother because you were working hard for the family, and she felt it wasn't fair to burden you with her troubles when they were only little things.

"The afternoon before, she'd run into a man who was a former client while she was out walking with Emily. He'd offered her a thousand dollars to spend a night with him, and the same again the next week for a second night. All she needed was for someone to mind Emily for the night.

"After thinking about it all the last night and that morning, she'd decided she'd do it. Two thousand dollars for two nights work would solve her money problems.

She said nobody ever needed to know, especially not you, Jim.

"She wanted to know if I'd mind you the following night because she knew it was my night off. If it worked out, she wanted me to do the same the next week.

"If I agreed, she'd drop you round the next evening and collect you on her way home in the early morning. You were a good sleeper, and she thought you'd sleep the whole night through without disturbing me, but she'd leave me a bottle just in case.

"I told her I thought it was a terrible idea. Your dad was … is a good man, and I told her once she started cheating on him it would be hard to stop. I knew as well that if he ever found out it would destroy what Cindy and he had together.

"I think she wanted me to talk her out of it, the way good friends do, but I could tell she was torn. The man who wanted to see her was decent and a good client from before, so she knew she'd be safe with him.

"I still said it was a bad idea. I asked her how she'd feel if Jim went off with another girl. She agreed she'd hate it, but didn't think he'd ever know. It was just her, with someone she'd already been with, one more time.

"I told her that was rubbish. Cheating was cheating. If she needed money for things then I'd help her.

"We talked back and forth for maybe an hour. In the end, it seemed I'd convinced her not to not do it. I gave her a hundred dollars and told her I'd give her more if she needed it. I told her to go and buy herself and Emily something nice.

"It was maybe eleven in the morning. She asked if I'd mind you for half an hour or so while she went out for a walk to clear her head to help her think straight. I told her to take as long as she needed.

"She thanked me for being a best friend. She promised she'd be back before long with some lunch for us to share.

"Before she left, she made me promise to never tell you what we'd talked about, Jim, even if she didn't go to bed with this man who'd offered her the money.

"I told her if something happened to her Jim would need to know, but she said she couldn't bear for you to know that she'd even considered it and she swore me to secrecy. She said she'd kill herself if you ever found out. She said she'd do this thing for me, that we'd made that blood promise. That's why, in the end, I reluctantly agreed.

"With my promise made, she walked out of the door. I never saw her again.

"When afternoon turned to evening, and she still hadn't come back, I got really worried. I had no milk for you, only a bottle of boiled water. And it wasn't like her to vanish. I took you out in the pram and walked the streets for an hour, asking if anybody had seen her, but nobody had. Then I had to go to work, so I bought a pint of milk, heated some in a bottle, fed you and you settled to sleep.

"As it was Monday, a quiet night, by midnight I was finished and came home to bed, hoping Cindy had returned, but there was still no sign.

"I slept badly, as did you. I think the cow's milk was upsetting you and giving you gripes. In the morning you had awful smelly diarrhoea and were very restless. I walked the streets again for a couple hours, but no matter where I went there was still no sign of Cindy.

"Finally, I remembered the drug dealer she used to buy from before. I went to ask him about Cindy because

I was starting to wonder if she'd taken the money I'd given her and gone to him for a fix.

"He was cagey when I saw him, but he finally admitted to seeing Cindy, although he said he hadn't talked to her. All he would say was that she'd called by and left again. He thought she'd left town and wouldn't be back again. I didn't for a minute believe him, but what more could I do.

"At that time, if I'd had your number, Jim, I might have rung you and asked you what to do, promise or no promise. But all I knew was you were working on a farm somewhere over the mountains.

"Meanwhile, I had a little baby who was getting sick and who I couldn't care for. You wouldn't eat or drink and still had diarrhoea. I could have taken you to the local doctor, but then I'd have had to explain the rest.

"Finally, I remembered I'd seen a hospital near a train station, the one just before Penrith, when I'd caught a train to the Blue Mountains once.

"Late in the afternoon, I caught the train there and checked it out. After dark, when nobody was around, I picked you out of your pram and carried you to near the front doors of the hospital.

"You'd finally settled, and I felt awful at the thought of leaving you, but I didn't know what else to do. So, I hid in the bushes and watched people coming and going for a while until I worked out a safe place to leave you just outside the doors. I knew someone would soon see you and bring you inside where they would look after you. There were some empty cardboard boxes in a pile outside a side door, so I lay you in one and carried it over to near the entrance and put you there.

"I watched from a distance, and at first you were quiet, but soon you started crying. An orderly heard you and came outside. He called for help, and a nurse came out and picked you up. I watched her carry you inside. I knew you'd be safe.

"It was my night off that night, and I walked the streets until dawn thinking that if I could only find Cindy, we could go together and rescue you. I looked everywhere I could think of, but there was still no sign. In the end, I gave up searching and went to sleep.

"It's been like an awful nightmare ever since, especially when you came home, Jim, and I couldn't tell you the little that I knew. I've tried my best to forget it ever happened, but it's not so easy."

Josephine stops talking and buries her hands in her face. Her body shakes in silent sobs.

I can't find it in me to be angry or bitter, only sad for us all. I reach out, take her hand, and pull her to me. I hold her for a long time before saying, "I don't blame you. You've carried your own guilt for far too long. Thank you for telling us what happened. At least now we know."

She wipes tears from her face and blows her nose, then gives us both a shaky smile and says, "I've thought it over so many times. The one person who I think knows more than he said is her drug dealer. I haven't seen him for a couple years, but I think I can find him. There never seemed any point in forcing the issue before; it was only for my own comfort. But if we go see him together, I'm sure we can find out the next part of Cindy's story."

Chapter 24 – Jim – Elusive Cindy

After a week, we've still been unable to locate the drug dealer Josephine told us about. She's put out feelers through her old friend network but got nothing back. Whether he's deliberately hiding or is no longer around, we don't know.

Because I don't have a full name or an address, or any way of being able to reach him, it all rests with Josephine. I trust she'll find him if he's still around. My memory of her from all those years ago was of her being attractive and classy, but she's so much more than that. She's educated and kind and competent in all she does. If anyone can find him, it's Josephine.

There was certainly a touch of sexual frisson between us back in those days before I met Cindy. But I'm surprised how much she appeals to me right now in deeper ways. I haven't seen her in person since last week, but I have spoken to her on the phone a few times, and I know Kate has called in to see her. In a very touching way, Josephine has become almost a substitute mother to Kate in the place of the one who vanished. I know she tells Kate stories of her mother that I never knew. I know it's something that means so very much to Kate.

In my conversations with Josephine, I've gained a bit of perspective. I always put Cindy in a gilded cage, thought of her as the perfect woman, almost a saintly virgin, though I knew from her past that was not so.

Violet's conversation, followed by Josephine's story, has forced me to see another side of her, that she was a woman with vulnerabilities, frailties and vanities, a good person but not the impossible saint I'd painted her as.

And who am I to judge. I've been far from perfect in my life. Why should I have ever expected her to be.

I also realise she was so young, far too young really for what was put upon her, to care for and support our child alone in my absence, with no other support and only the paltry amount of money I'd left her.

Yes, Josephine wasn't far away, but since I'd pulled Cindy out of her former life, their friendship had weakened, even though she went to see her in final desperation at the end. I see now she needed the daily companionship of others in her life. Most people have parents, siblings, cousins and a network of friends who form a support network in their lives. When Cindy came to be with me, she gave all that up and was left trying to cope alone.

My conversations with Josephine have made me feel a bit ashamed of my own lack of seeing, but then I was as young and naive as she was. Nobody had shown either of us any rule book to live by.

I know now, in my heart, that Cindy is dead, that she died many years ago. She would never have abandoned her baby if she was alive. Is it better she didn't leave me for another? In truth I don't know.

A second week elapses without further news.

Perhaps it's time to face the reality that Cindy's final story is unknowable. I've done little else in the past two weeks. I've haven't even told Kate of my discovery below my house, and she hasn't asked. I've done odd jobs for a few dollars here and there and read some old books, but nothing more.

Now I think it's finally time to move my life along.

My phone rings. It's her. Josephine. "Hello."

Her voice, breathless, comes down the line. "Jim, I think I've found him. I called you first."

"What does think mean?"

"A source of a source thinks he saw him last night. They say he's scared of something or someone, and that he's keeping real low."

We make a plan to wait tonight where he was seen last night, at a back-street diner, a place where a lot of drug users go to eat or collect. It's not that we expect to see him, but we hope to get in contact with the person who saw him last night and this person will know where he went.

I stock up on hard dollars of the green and yellow kind, as Josephine says the information will cost us. We settle in the diner like an old married couple, sharing a meal and partaking of wine. An hour passes slowly as does another.

The owner knows why we're waiting and keeps watch. Perhaps, nothing will happen, but here we must stay. As the clock passes nine and draws closer to ten, the owner draws our attention with a nod of his head. He indicates a woman with a pock-marked face and a hard demeanour. She slips into a booth and sits heavily.

Josephine places a hand on my arm to keep me seated. She rises and saunters over to the counter, dropping her glove as she passes the woman. The woman picks it up and calls out, waves it for attention. When Josephine goes to take it from her, something is exchanged both ways.

Josephine nods her thanks and comes back to our table. As she sits she shows me what she was passed. It's a small business card with the name, number and address of our next contact point.

We pay our bill, leaving a generous tip to both parties, and leave. As we walk along the street, Josephine takes my hand in hers. We walk this way until we turn a corner, when we separate. I look across at her and she gives me a look of affection. I put my hand on her shoulder. She in return slides her body against mine.

To anyone watching us, we're just a middle-aged married couple going home after dinner. I know it's for cover, but the feeling of being near to Josephine like this is really good. She slides her hand around my waist, and I pull her in tight.

We walk in silence until we round the next corner, then she turns to face me with an enigmatic half smile. "I'm so glad you found me. I like being with you very much. I'd forgotten how much. Why don't we leave this for the night? We have a number to let us continue our search again tomorrow. For the rest of tonight you could put your shoes alongside mine?"

In barely an hour, her body is joined to mine. "You know I always fancied you," she says later as we lie together. "If I hadn't had to work that night when we'd agreed to meet, you'd never have met Cindy. It's really weird to think of. Oh, god that sounds terrible.

"I never begrudged Cindy for taking you or having your child. I guess it just wasn't meant to be back then, if you believe in that kind of thing. I love that you and Kate are in my life again now. It's like a double blessing.

"And I want you to know that I haven't lived one day since I left Kate outside that hospital without grieving her absence and wishing I'd made a different choice. Giving her away filled me with as much guilt as if I'd given up my own child. I should have found a way to keep her, return her to you when you came back."

I pull her in close to me and nuzzle my face into her hair. I say, "Yes, it's kind of strange, I did not understand much about the ways of women back then, but wondered if that was what you were offering.

"I thought you far too beautiful to be interested in me, but yet I was drawn to you back then. And then of course I met Cindy and forgot about everything else. But I'm just glad to be here with you now."

As we talk more, she tells me of her years of loveless marriage, rich in money but poor in every other way.

Then she jokes and says, "You know, to become your woman, I've always had to take the initiative. I knew back then, when I first met you, that you liked me but were too shy to act on it. I thought it could end up the same again this time if I didn't act first. For a fortnight, I waited and hoped you'd ring me and arrange to meet, just the two of us.

"Kate had no such hesitation. We've become the best of friends. She even confided to me that she thought you needed a good woman, and she hoped I would be the one.

"I know I'll never replace the love you felt for Cindy. I just hope this feels good and right for you as it does for me."

I say, "I'm wonderfully happy in this place with you. There's nowhere else I'd rather be."

We make love again, and it's even better than before. In whatever form it takes, I hope Josephine will stay in our lives forever. It's clear though that to move forwards, we need to lay past ghosts to rest.

What we must do is find the long-lost Cindy.

The next day, we begin our search in earnest, seeking Cindy's elusive drug dealer and through him Cindy. It takes a week and two thousand dollars of our cash, and assurances given that we are not the police or a rival drug gang, but we finally set up a meeting with him.

Kate's now involved. We've agreed we'll keep no secrets from her, including about our own togetherness.

When we told her, she gave us both a joyous hug and said, "I know I won't get a fairy tale ending where I bring my birth father and mother back together after all these years, but having the two of you in that role feels equally wonderful."

It's early afternoon when we meet the man who might finally be able to tell us what happened to Cindy. He now operates in a seedier part of Sydney than he did thirty years ago, out of a dingy flat at the back of Cabramatta. We don't meet him there but in a small restaurant around the corner, from which he does many of his drug deals.

He's already seated when we walk in, and when he sees Kate, his face goes white, as if he's seen a ghost. I suppose he has really. She grows more like her mother with every passing day now that Josephine is helping her choose clothes and make up. Her taste and her mothers are like identical twins, and Josephine's memories provide the link between the two.

After that, getting the real story is easy. He remembers that day well. He'd gone out to do a drug delivery in the morning. While he was out, Cindy, who knew the way to his place and where he kept his stash, put the hundred dollars from Josephine on the table as payment and injected herself with what she thought was a standard dose of heroin.

"She didn't know it was an extra strong batch. I don't know if she'd been buying from someone else, but she hadn't bought from me in over a year. Guess her tolerance would have been low.

"She was warm when I found her. The needle was still in her arm. She must have blacked out quickly. I swear I checked and checked for a pulse. She was gone.

It's funny, for me hearing this news is almost a relief, not that I want her dead, anything but, yet the story of a sudden and peaceful end is so much better than many alternatives I've imagined. Still the certainty it brings is shattering in its own way, it is one thing to think something is so, another entirely when all doubt and hope has vanished.

I look at Jo, this news has hit her hard, her hands are covering her face in anguish. Reality tears at her too.

Kate has looked away, I am unable to see her eyes, but the strain in her neck and face, an emotion of holding back any outward display, is clear in what it says.

I ask the man to continue, I want to hear the story to its end, to know what became of her after.

I say, "What then?'

He goes on,"I couldn't call the cops and end up in jail, and I didn't want to just dump her in the harbour. I had a delivery to Newcastle that night, so I took her. On the way, near Ourimbah, I bought a tracksuit and pants from a disposals shop, the kind the people who buy from me wear. If I'd left her dressed nice the cops might have tried extra hard to find an identity, you know with public appeals and all that. Instead, if she looked like a down and out druggie, I figured they wouldn't make more than a quick effort. I threw her nice clothes in a waste bin and took her to this place where people go to score hits. People die there sometimes. I left the syringe she'd used next to her, did my other business and drove back to Sydney.

"Guess it worked, cos I never heard any more about her. Well, not apart from when you came by and asked me about her," he says to Josephine. "I'm really sorry for all that happened and that I couldn't tell you."

We all sit there is stunned silence, there is nothing to say that will bring Cindy back.

I know it will be relatively simple to find her final resting place. We can confirm her identity with Kate's DNA if needed. I doubt we will.

I stand up and nod my thanks as we leave.

Chapter 25 – Josephine – Requiem Cindy

I'm standing at Cindy's grave in Newcastle's Honeysuckle Cemetery, wondering where more than three decades have gone since we were carefree teenagers together.

Her grave was unmarked until today, when the name I knew her by, Lucinda McGrevy, was added. She'll always be Cindy to me. She'll always be my best friend.

I have no tears left to cry, but a heaviness sits in my heart. I remember her carefree teenage spirit so clearly, her brown hair and flashing dark eyes, always tinged with mischief. She was always the game one and good for a dare.

There was that night when I dared her to go talk to Jim when I couldn't make it. He was tall and handsome with dark wavy hair, a boy fresh out of the country with dirt under his nails. He had one of those well-muscled torsos that come with hard manual work. He'd told me he was a gardener and machine driver at Centennial Park, as well as doing odd jobs here and there.

None of those things made him utterly delectable; what made him utterly delectable was his shy naivety. I don't think he'd ever held a girl's hand before, let alone touched or kissed one.

On a whim I decided I wanted to be his first. You'd never noticed him and he'd never seen you. I planned my seduction, he was keen if green, not knowing what I offered but knowing it would be a thrill. I asked him to wait for me outside. I could see him through the window down there.

But a very rich man offered a large sum of money to have me for the full night so I could not leave. As a dare,

I sent you instead. My plan was for you to get him for a night and my turn would come next.

I never dreamed it would be love at first sight, that you two would become inseparable, that by the next day he would have so entranced you that you'd come back together to announce to Lulu that your days as a street girl were over.

It was like a fairy tale. Soon you were walking around proudly, with your big belly, and then you were pushing a tiny baby in a pram.

You and Jim had your eyes in the stars, your life was all planned. I so envied your happiness. I never let my jealousy show, or ever hinted I fancied him too. But he had an aura about him. It was magnetic.

I'm so sorry, Cindy; I should have minded you better. I shouldn't have felt envy for you that day when you came with your tiny baby. You told me about your troubles, and I couldn't bear the idea that you'd cheat on Jim. It would smash a fairy tale. But I liked the idea of taking your place as surrogate mother to this little baby, if just for an hour or two. She was beautiful like you. I was bewitched with her, just as I was with you.

We'd been instant best friends from the first moment we met, me fresh out of Wagga, the blond daughter of a drunk shearer, the girl all the other lads in the shed tried to feel up when her father was too drunk to notice.

A few succeeded. By the age of fifteen, I'd made a bed up in the back of the wool bales. I'd give them what they wanted for a ten dollar note. When I had fifty notes saved, I caught a train to Sydney to make my own way in the world.

I was sitting in the street on that first day in Sydney when I saw you, not far from Redfern station. You sat next to me and told me your foster father had belted you and given you that big black eye. You also told me how he held you down when his wife went out and did whatever he wanted to you. Whenever you tried to fight back, he would hit you in the face, the way he had done earlier that day.

I told you not to cop that shit, to come with me instead. I had money. We'd get our own place, a place where people paid us to do those things, not take them from us for free.

And that's what we did. At first it was just us, doing it alone, but then we met Lulu. After that it was easy money, safer than being out on our own. Along the way we tried a few drugs, but they never really got hold of me the way they got hold of you. Sometimes, I had to drag you out of the gutter and bring you home.

I knew why. Drugs helped you forget all you'd had to endure. You were more fragile that way. Me, I could let the men we were with happen and straightaway forget them, knowing life would soon move on again and all would be fine. You were never that way.

But we were tight. We laughed, joked and played together. We had each other's back. Early on, we made a blood promise together. We would stay best friends forever and look after each other. We were sixteen when we made our promise.

It always held, right up until that last day.

That day I knew your life was unravelling. I should have minded you back then, more than ever, but I did not. Instead of letting you go off on your own, I should have gone with you, taken you shopping, bought new clothes for you and Emily. We could have shared a nice lunch together. I should have made you to stay over with me until Jim came back. Instead, I wanted to play Mummy with Emily.

I remember my pleasure as she gooed and gaaed in my arms. How I walked down the street with her in the pram, showing her off as if she were mine. I forgot your needs in my moment of gloating and pleasure.

Half my mind knew you could shoot up. It had always been your escape route from before. So, at first, when you didn't return, I thought you were probably drugged, maybe drunk, maybe even getting laid in a drunken stupor.

Despite my protests to you, I didn't even mind that idea so much. It was only sex, after all. We had done it with endless men, so what was another time. I didn't really believe that another one-night fuck mattered so much, except that it was cheating on the Jim and Cinderella fairy tale. If this fairy tale could come true for you, then, maybe, one day, it could for me too.

If I'd cared enough, I'd have gone looking for you straight after lunch. I'd have found you on the floor, maybe out to it, but still alive. The ambulance would have come; they'd have stuck a needle in you and brought you back to life like they had once before when you'd had too much.

Instead, I left you to die alone, and I did not like being Mummy anymore.

When it was too late, I cared and I searched.

Now, our smiles and laughter together can only ever live in my mind. And I am so sad. I miss you so much. If only it was me in this grave, not you. Instead, I'm here. I have your Jim and your grown-up baby, but what I most want is you.

In the last month of playing happy families with Jim and Kate, I have been living a lie, pretending to be you, as if pretending could somehow make it true. I can't live like this any longer. The dream is over.

In the morning, I'll be gone. I don't know where, and I don't know if I'll return. I need to find myself and seek forgiveness from you. I hope Jim and Kate will understand and one day forgive me too.

Chapter 26 – Kate – Losing and Searching

Josephine leaving Jim is almost the cruellest blow. I know of his devastation when he lost my mother and me. But back then he was young and resilient and made a new life for himself out west.

His happiness with Josephine, in their short time together was clear.To find a new life with another, along with finally finding me and knowing what happened to my mother was something good. I could feel his happiness in those few short days. He walked around whistling, hands in his pockets, as if life was fresh and bright again, a diamond that sparkled.

Since Josephine left the whistling is gone.

He just mooches aimlessly.

It was hard for him discovering what happened to my mother, even harder for me. I'd always kept a fairy tale version of her alive inside my head. One day she would come out of nowhere. She would suddenly return and reclaim me, explain it was a mistake and now she was back. There was no logic in this fairy tale, but my heart kept the image bright.

But when we heard the story, then came to Newcastle, saw the old records and got the results from the DNA test which I demanded, I had no choice but to let my fairy tale die with my mother.

It was different for Jim. He'd known in his heart Cindy was no longer alive. So, on that day in Newcastle, it was like he was given permission to let his last hope go and share his pain with Josephine. She was a new beautiful person who connected him with that long-lost past but also brought him alive in the present in a way that allowed him to leave that distant pain behind. Her leaving without any explanation of where or why was the cruellest blow.

I can't blame her. She carries blame enough for two.

I want Josephine back too. For just a brief moment the three of us were a family made anew. Through her shared connection and distant history, she feels like another version of the first mother I never knew.

Now she's punishing herself for that past, I think she doesn't feel she is entitled to this new and unexpected happiness she's found with me and Jim, or that she can be a substitute for my mother.

My father would never have asked her to stay if he'd known she was leaving. He's lost far too much before and is too proud to beg.

I know what I must do. I must rebuild my father like a work of clay, give him a new purpose in life to start each day. And maybe, in time, when he grows strong enough, he can find and bring Josephine back.

She's beautiful and kind, and through her memories and friendship from that time long ago, she carries part of my mother's essence on through time. It's the closest I will ever get to my mother, and that's enough for me.

But we're both here without her for now, and I know my father needs to gain back his own sense of worth. Helping him discover the history of his house is a way I can help him find a renewed purpose. If he can discover it's untold and long-hidden story, he'll find a purpose in doing something he enjoys and become a part of its history too.

I've already done a little research, and I now know the quarry marks on the stones are the marks of the Irish Brothers, a gang of three, who, under the direction of James Greenway, did much of the building of the

Government Stables in the 1820s, that fantastic building that's now the modern day Conservatorium of Music.

I suspect Jim's house was built by one of these men for himself. It's lucky Jim's purchase and sharp observations preserved the house and uncovered the first part of its story. Jim has rescued a national treasure, a thing beyond price.

The house is a fitting epithet for such an unassuming man. I think when Jim grows large in the confidence that uncovering and protecting the history of this house will bring, he'll be ready to search for Josephine and bring her back to our lives. It's my hope.

In the period after we found Josephine, but before we found my mother, Jim relaid the floor and moved his furniture back in. When I asked why, he said he wanted his house back the way it was.

He's done it expertly, so precisely, that anyone would be hard pressed to notice the flagstones had ever been lifted. I absolutely can't fault the workmanship, but I wish he'd waited until we'd finished our exploration.

I can't force Jim to resume unearthing the history of the house, but if I can persuade him we should work together to excavate the area below the floor, my sixth sense tells me it will reveal the lost story of how this house came to be.

Tonight, despite Jim's new reluctance to go out, I've persuaded him to come for dinner with me and my mum and dad. He and my dad have become good friends, so I've primed Dad to get him to tell us the story of the house, how he bought it, and what we found below the floor. Hopefully, the conversation will renew Jim's interest in continuing a joint investigation. I don't know why he seems cagey about this of late. I wonder if he found something he doesn't want me to know about, and that's why he relaid the floor.

If he won't agree to continuing the house project, my next best alternative to give him a purpose is for the two of us to work together in tracing his mother's family and my mother's family. There'll surely be information to be found, and I like the idea of working alongside him to ferret it out.

I suspect it doesn't matter what our first project is, only that we get active and do something together to pull him out of his blues.

I haven't told him I have an email address for Josephine, and I plan to send her an email of our news every couple weeks so she doesn't forget about us and what's happening here. I know I'm selfish, but I don't want her to get attached to somebody else or to some other place.

At dinner, Dad and I broach the investigation of the house with Jim. I tell him about the Irish brothers and their mason's mark, and I see a spark of interest in his eyes, but he's still resistant to the idea of opening up below. But, surprisingly, he's pleasantly receptive to the idea of tracing our family history.

When the meal is done, the four of us sit around the dining table with a coffee and a glass of port, one of Dad's ongoing family traditions, which Jim is happy to partake in.

Jim tells us the fragments he knows about his own life, his unknown father, his mother, who he knows was adopted many years ago from an unknown person in Sydney. His mother's name was Rachel Martin, but whether that was an adoptive name or her birth name he has no idea.

From the tiny bits she told Jim, her childhood memories were anything but happy and, like Cindy, she left home as soon as she was able. In her case she went to the country where she found work as a domestic in the house of a wealthy farming family on a sheep property out from Moree.

It seems that while she was there, the son of the family took a fancy to her and harassed her with unwanted attention. To escape him, she moved to a small town further out where the farming industry was a mix of sheep and crops. Before long, she was pregnant to an itinerant shearer. That's all Jim knows of his father, but it seems the town his mother moved to cared for its own, and so she stayed on and made it her home.

Jim says, "She refused to tell me anything about my father except he was a shearer who went from town to town. As child I never really asked. I'm not sure if I ever saw him, and if I did, I never knew who he was.

"My mother had no time for him, called him a deadbeat who she was stupid enough to let touch her. I never even knew his name. She said that when she told him she was pregnant with me, he said he wanted nothing to do with it, so she told him to fuck off and never spoke to him again.

"As a child, I took her at her word and left it at that. It was just the two of us living in a tiny weatherboard cottage on the outskirts of town, not in the black's camp, but not far away. She paid rent each week to a business in town that owned our house. The landlord was a local shopkeeper.

"Her work in the town was a mixture of bar and domestic work for families, cleaning, cooking, that sort of thing. I think people liked her because a few came to her funeral and some business owners put in money to pay for her burial and gravestone. She got sick with ovarian cancer when I was about fifteen. They operated, but it did no good, and she died about a year later.

"I worked from when I was ten, doing anything I could to earn dollars and contribute to our living costs. She said we both had to do our share.

"When she was sick, a few people offered her charity, but she wouldn't accept it and, for the last months before she died, we lived off her savings and little bits of money I earned. We had just enough to pay the last rent. It covered up to the weekend after she died, with about fifty dollars left in the money tin to cover odds and ends.

"She told me to take whatever money was left and go to Sydney once she died. She wanted me to make a new life for myself out of that Godforsaken town, as she called it.

"So, I did. I've never been back since. I suppose people in town knew more of her than I did, maybe they even knew who my father was."

"Did your mum have any brothers of sisters," I ask him. "Who was the person who left you the money to fix up the house when she died?"

Jim's not really sure and never inquired. He got a letter from a solicitor in Brisbane with a cheque attached which said it was from the sale of the estate of his aunt. He presumes it was from his mother's sister, who'd written once.

"My mother didn't really mention her, only that she was hoity-toity and lived in Brisbane with her husband, some rich dude. I suppose I could find the solicitor's letter, maybe get some more information about my mother that way."

My Dad's a retired accountant who knows about these things says, "If you give me a copy of the letter, I'll ring the solicitor's firm in Brisbane to seek details about the family. We could take a visit to Brisbane the weekend after next. We're overdue a visit there. We could all travel there for a couple days to meet whoever we can locate. Your aunt may well have had children of her own."

My dad is a master of organisation, and that next Friday night, we all fly to Queensland. He's arranged for us to visit the oldest daughter of Jim's deceased aunt. She's apparently in her fifties and knows little of her mother's life before marriage, but she's happy to try and help.

We meet at a café in New Farm for brunch. It's a lovely location which looks out over the Brisbane River. She's a friendly open woman called Sharon, and she chats away comfortably with us for ten minutes over coffee before she pulls out a sheaf of papers. "My father died a decade ago. His was an old moneyed Brisbane family who've lived in the area since the early days."

She looks at Jim. "My mother though, that's your Aunt Jane, came here when she was seven, first as a foster child. She was soon adopted by her foster parents, who were also well to do Brisbane people.

"She had a happy life with her new family, and studied music, dancing and art. In time she became a musician of note. That's when she met and married my dad. I'm the eldest of her five children.

"She appointed me as the executor of her estate at the end when her health failed. I did try, in those final days, to get her to talk of her childhood, but she said she remembered little because she was taken into care so young. She did know she had a little sister, your mum, but for years she never knew what had become of her. That was until the year after she got married when she was pregnant and had free time on her hands. Then she managed to find where Rachel was.

"She sent your mum a letter, with a hundred dollars and a photo of herself, and invited her to come and visit them in Brisbane. She offered to pay for the trip if needed. Two months later she got a short sharp letter back with a picture of my Aunt Rachel and you, James. The hundred dollars was returned. Rachel said she'd much rather earn her own money than take gifts from strangers, and so she turned down the offer of the trip.

"My mum was mortified and never tried to contact Rachel again. Instead, she opened a bank account in your name. For the next ten years she paid money into it, thinking that, when you came of age, it might help you and be a step towards building a bridge back to Rachel.

"She found out that your mum had died when a welfare officer contacted her about you because you were only sixteen and might need care. She offered to take care of you if you came to Brisbane, but by then you'd vanished and they couldn't locate you.

"So she moved the money she'd saved for you into an investment account, and it stayed there and slowly increased until she died.

"As executor of the estate, I was luckily able to locate you, eventually, to give you the money she'd put aside for you. That's all I know really.

"I have the old letter and photo exchange in my mum's things, as well as a photo of her and her sister when they were little together. I also have my mum's original birth and marriage certificates. They gave me some early details of where she was born and who her birth parents were." Sharon pauses speaking and takes some things from her handbag.

She passes the first Jim. He looks at it intently, as if torn back in time. It is a black and white photo of small boy and his mother standing outside a shabby old timber house, both proudly gazing at the camera, as if rich beyond measure.

Sharon then passes on a second photograph from an even earlier time of two little girls, arms around each other, smiling at a camera. She says, "My mother said that photo was taken just before they were put into foster care."

I look from Jim to the old photographs, feeling a flood of emotion wash over me. They are the smallest records of vanished lives, but it's something more than the nothing we've ever had before.

Chapter 27 – Jim – A Starting Place

Sharon shows us an old and faded photo of me and my mother taken in front of our house a lifetime ago when I was eight. I'd forgotten how shabby it was. Even in the photo, you can see the collapsing picket fence, broken front steps and cracks in the cement path leading to the door. But it was our home, and we loved it. Later, when I got handy with tools, I repaired these things and made it look better with a new coat of paint.

In the photo, I'm a proud eight-year-old bursting with life, my mother's arm around my shoulder. We are both happy in that time and place.

I'd forgotten how beautiful my mother was before she got sick. She's radiant and lovely with her long dark hair and delicate pretty features, something like a fierce bird, proud and possessive but kind looking too.

It's good to see her when she was still well, before cancer ate her away and she was not much more than a shell around bones. I would pick her up and carry her in and out of the house, and she weighed almost nothing, felt as though a puff of wind would blow her away.

Here she looks pleased with what we have: clean clothes, a house of our own, enough food for us both, and the joy of watching as her small garden grows. She would say those things were all she wanted and, with these things, she had made a simple but good life. She told me often she was happy with just me.

Tears prick at the back of my eyelids as the photo takes me back in time. A vast sense of loss for the mother I'd almost forgotten surfaces.

Then comes a second photo of two little girls, captured in a moment of together happiness, before their lives were torn away. It's incredibly poingnant to see a time when they were still best friends, unaware of what was to come.

Kate rests her hand on my arm and gives it a gentle squeeze. I'm so blessed to have this woman as my daughter, grandchild of the woman she never had the chance to know, who now stares out of the picture.

I pass the photos back to Sharon. "Would you be able to get me a copy of these, please?"

She hands them back to me. "They are yours to keep. And I have this to give you too." She passes me a copy of her mother's birth certificate. It has the name of Jane's mother, Rosalie Martin, along with the statement, 'Father Unknown'. Rosalie's age at the time of Jane's birth is twenty-four and the place of birth is the Royal Prince Alfred Hospital in Camperdown. This means that Rosalie was twenty-six when my mother was born.

So, Martin is our real family name, not the one given to my mother at adoption. I wonder if anyone knew who my grandfather was back then. I suspect not. It seems to be a pattern that repeats. It makes me sad, Kate became the third generation of fatherless children, until we found each other.

With the name of my grandmother now known, I assume I'll easily be able to get a copy of my mother's birth certificate, a first step towards finding her past.

I go to put the photos and birth certificate away. As I do I see a note on the back of the earlier photo, in small hand writing saying, 'Taken at' then listing a street address in Redfern.

Seeing these documents stirs a distant memory of a small leather case, like a miniature suitcase, that my mother kept under her bed. It was the place where she kept bills and papers. I never gave any thought to my mother's personal things when I left the house all those years ago. I just walked out to catch the train. Someone else, most likely the landlord, must have gone through the residue of my mother's life. I wonder if they still have any of her things.

Maybe they consigned them to a bin or burnt them in a backyard pile. Their value was negligible, but I see now they are the final fragments that may tell of her life before me. I'd like to know what became of them, even if it means going back to that empty place with its memories of loss, that I've never wanted to return to.

That night, we dine with Sharon's family. Kate is joyous to discover an aunt she never knew. Sharon's children, of a similar age to Kate, are there too. They all laugh and chat, nineteen to the dozen, as they sit around the dinner table.

I love seeing Kate happy with her new family, but it's also bittersweet, decades of loss, years thrown away, a family I never knew. What could have made my mother so proud and angry, making her despise and reject help offered in kindness by her own sister.

We fly back to Sydney the next day, and Kate sits beside me. She asks to see the photo of her grandmother, Rachel, again. I pull the things from Sharon out and hand the photo to her. I'm left with the copy of my Aunt Jane's birth certificate and the second photo of the two little girls.

I look again. There's something jangling in the back of my mind. I study this photo closely and then turn it over and look at the writing on the back. My eyes notice a familiar address. I'm almost certain it's the same address as the one on the contract of sale of my house, the listed address of my home's last registered owner. It's a Redfern street address. Could the former owner of my house have lived at the Redfern address, or perhaps next door. It's hard to remember if the street number on the sale contract was forty-two or forty-four.

It's then I think of Sharon. From the moment we met I had a sense of familiarity. She couldn't have been the woman who sold me my house, as that person would be much older by now. But, if I recall the image of that woman back into my memory, she could be Sharon's sister their appearance is definitely similar.

I try to recall her name. Perhaps the contract says Elouise. I know the surname is definitely Rossi, which sounds Italian rather than Anglo-Saxon.

The idea of a family connection there, somewhere, seems most unlikely, yet feels plausible. One more thing to try and find out. I won't tell Kate and raise her hopes with another wild goose chase. This mystery is mine to follow up. I'll find the sale contract and check that address tomorrow. If the address matches, I'll go there and knock on the door myself.

The following morning after breakfast, I find the relevant sale documents. My memory was right; the former owner of my house lives at No 44. The address written on the photo of my mother and her sister is No 42. Right next door.

I visit at lunch time, a good time to find an older person at home. The two houses are amazingly alike, as if they're a pigeon pair that were built together.

I start with No 44. A young woman, perhaps around Kate's age, answers. There's no family resemblance, and she's not overly friendly, but I tell her my story anyway.

"I'm trying to locate the owner of a house I bought from a person who lived here about thirty years ago. Her name was Elouise Rossi."

She clearly knows who I mean though she says nothing at first, just screws up her face as if thinking. "Oh, you mean that old dump of a place between the railway lines. Yes, I was a kid when it was sold, but I remember it. My mother, Ellie by the way, not Elouise, took me there one time. It wasn't much to look at, but it was kind of cute, I guess."

As if making up her mind to be friendlier, she holds out her hand. "I'm Marti, Ellie's daughter."

"Does she still live here?"

She nods.

"Do you think she'd be willing to meet me?"

Another nod. "Maybe later though. She's napping."

"When would be a good time to come back?"

She pauses and seems to think more before she finally says, "I expect her to wake soon. Tis only a morning nap, so you could come back in half an hour."

After another pause where she maybe considers a true effort to be hospitable, her politeness wins. "Well, scrap that. Why don't we have a cuppa and I'll call her. She loves a cuppa after her nap. It's as good a time as any for a chat."

We sit and talk for half an hour until her mother eventually joins us. I doubt she'll remember me, but she does right away. She's seems amazingly observant.

I've planned out what I want to know, a list of things: how long she's lived here, if she knows this house's history, why and how she came by the house she sold to me, and if she knows anything of people who owned the house next door over fifty years ago. The thing I want to know the most is the last thing, but it's best to begin with the others. They seem less nosey.

I tell Ellie and Marti about the discoveries I made in my house when I started digging up the floor, of the hidden basement and early stonemason marks. I don't give too much detail, just say there was floor below the actual floor, and it covered the top of old stairs I'm yet to explore.

"Before I decide whether to go digging, which I'm told needs an archaeologist's permit and costs lots of money, I'm trying to find out anything known about the house's history and past owners."

Ellie is a bit hazy about some details, but she knows the general story of my house. "It's been in the family for as long as anyone knows, for at least a hundred years. It was my great-grandmother's. She died of the Spanish flu in 1918 when she was forty, and after that a son lived there, one of Ellie's great-uncles, until the Great Depression. He eventually abandoned the house to go off looking for work across the outback, and he never came back. It was said he enlisted in the Second World War and died in a Japanese labour camp. After that the house notionally belonged to my mother who never did anything with it. She passed in the late 1970s. That's when I sold the place."

She winks at me and says, "I could see you were desperate to have it, lad. I might've sold it for less at the time, but then I think you've done well enough in the long run, the way all Sydney property prices have risen."

I smile in agreement. "Well, you're right there. It's worth plenty more now than when I bought it."

It feels like we're co-conspirators, and I can see Marti, is enjoying the banter too. We're all grinning at our in-joke. It seems like a natural moment to ask about the history of this house. "Sounds like you've lived here for a long time to know all that. Was this house a family heirloom too?"

She tells me a story of two sisters who bought side by side land parcels and of their builder husbands, Marco and Pietro Rossi, who were brothers and who built the two houses as mirror images.

"The houses were built in the 1890s, at the end of the Victorian era. Over the years, the family's fortunes in the two houses had diverged. Any family connection between the two houses is long gone now. No 44 has been sold and had new owners three times over the last fifty years. In fact, it's vacant again now and soon to be sold. The owners have moved interstate to be closer to their grandkids. I'm helping them, popping in to check on it and keep the gardens watered until the sale's done in a couple months' time. Just now builders are putting in a new kitchen and bathroom to up the sale value."

She looks at Marti and says, "I need to water the garden today, actually, so why don't you get the keys."

She turns to me. "If you want, Jim, I'll show you around. I know the owners won't mind."

I follow Ellie and Marti, wh unlocks garden gate then leaves us to go inside on our own. Ellie may be pushing eighty, but she's remarkably sprightly, walking quickly and with clear purpose.

We enter a side gate that leads to the back garden. At first glance, I'm blown away. It's like a palace garden, a hidden treasure. It's surprisingly deep and has been terraced over three levels, with the lowest level nestled behind the back door like a fairy grotto, full of ferns around a cascading water feature, pools, rockeries and a tiny flowing waterfall tumbling in the far corner, where it exits from the mouth of a sculpted fish. Coloured fish swim in the pool below.

The next level is a paved courtyard area. It sits under the shelter of a mass of flowering stone fruit trees such as cherry blossoms. Cushioned benches, small tables and relaxing chairs are arranged around the outside of a central knurled cherry blossom tree, its trunk a foot thick with widespread branches providing a canopy across most of the courtyard. It's awash in pale pink flowers. At the edge of a square of paving more similarly aged stone fruit trees tower over the space adding their own floral colour. The scent and hues of fallen flowers make this place feel like one has entered a soft lighted fairy palace.

The furthest back level is up a flight of six steps, which lead into a sun-drenched flower garden. Flowers of all conceivable shapes and colours grow here in bright sunlight. A narrow, park-like bench and a table sit in the centre, surrounded by the raised flower beds. It's all an overwhelming visual delight, and I must be standing with my mouth open.

Ellie gives a half cackle. "Quite something, isn't it?"

"Did the current owners design the garden?"

"Oh, no, it was the work of my great-grandfather and his brother and their wives. The men came out from Italy as labourers who'd worked for a grand manor with a garden something like this back there. They sought to recreate it here. This was their work of art, an attempt at a northern Italian palazzo in their own home.

"Our garden is nice, but it doesn't have this grandeur. Luckily, the current owners are keen gardeners. They fell in love with this place because of this garden, and they've beautifully maintained it since, but they've just kept what was already here. It was quite neglected when they bought it.

I only wish I had the money to buy it and bring the house back into the family, but I don't, so I'm hoping the new owners will treat it with the love it deserves."

She unwinds a hose with a soft spray nozzle and spends a few minutes caressing flowers with soft water. When she's finished, she winds it away and says, "Come inside. I need to check what the builders have done."

I follow her as she does a quick check of the bathroom, which elicits a small smile of satisfaction. She moves into the kitchen where a grimace is evident, though the reason escapes me. I suspect an argument over details with a busy builder is likely to follow.

"While we're here, I should give you a quick guided tour." she says.

It's a beautiful house, full of tastefully constructed details, which any lover of fine buildings would surely admire. We pass quickly from room to room until we come to an alcove room under the eaves at the top of the house, which has a view out the back over the delightful garden. It's obviously been set up as a kids' room with two little beds either side of the window.

Under the window is a thing that takes all my breath away. It's an armoire, and painted on it is a perfect reproduction of something I saw in a photo as a child, so very distantly remembered and yet perfectly sharp.

My mother had a scrapbook where she pasted pictures of things that appealed to her. She was always adding to it, just odd bits and pieces, cut-outs from magazines and newspapers. Glued to the inside cover was a photograph of a marvellous armoire with an ornate intricate carving, beautifully done. But its most striking feature was a hand-painted picture of two brightly coloured birds facing each other. Even in my mother's ancient photograph the detail was perfect, two red and a yellow lorikeets each chewing opposite sides of a pine cone that hung between them. It was striking then, and its real-life reproduction is even more striking now. I stand and point, mouth open but speechless.

Ellie nods and smiles a smile of secret enjoyment or something similar. "Yes, it really is striking. My great aunt was a very talented painter. She drew its outline by hand and then painted in all the detail before it was sealed under a layer of lacquer to preserve it.

"But this picture was in the front of my mother's scrap book. How did it get there?"

Now Ellie looks puzzled. "Are you sure it's the same picture? I've never seen another like it, and as far as I know it's the only one. My great aunt drew her first version based on two birds she saw feeding in the nearby park, sharing a pine cone from opposite sides. She took her hand drawing and made a tracing of it which is here, copied from the first but much more detailed drawing.

I'm sure I have the original drawing in her papers. I'll look if you like. She drew it over a hundred years ago, yet the colour is as brilliant today as then."

I start to try explain, but it's all such a jumble, then I remember the picture of my mother and her sister that I have with me. I show it to Ellie. "That was my mother. She's been dead for many years now."

Now Ellie's hand goes to her mouth, "Oh, my God, that's a picture of my cousins, Jane and Rachel. They were only four and six when I last saw them. I was best friends with Jane, we were the same age. Even though we were all only small children back then, I'd know them both anywhere, my mind image is still so clear.

"Rachel and my younger sister Barbara were also of an age and were like two peas in a pod. Most people thought they were identical twins, even though they were cousins.

I take out the other photo and Jane's birth certificate and explain my other purpose, to try and find out where my mother came from.

We sit side by side on one of the narrow beds as I continue to stare at the amazing real life image that I first saw in a scrap book decades ago.

I see Ellie staring intently at the photo of my mother as an adult. She says, "Looking at this photo, I can see your mother grew into the same likeness of Barbara as an adult. It's thirty-five years since Barbara died, God rest her soul. I miss her yet.

I ask, "Do you know what happened to my mother and sister, why they were taken away? It seems they were happy here. What went wrong?

Ellie pauses to gather her thoughts, "It was quite a story. It was said they were being abused, so Jane and Rachel were taken away, adopted out they said. We tried to find them, but nobody would allow us to know where they went.

"My mother would have gladly taken them both in if she could have found them. But all they would tell us was they'd gone for adoption, and would be much better off that way.

"The welfare people said it was unfair on them as children, and on their new parents, for them to be contacted and pulled back to their past, that some things are best left behind. They would never say exactly what those things were, but it seemed there was some sort of child abuse, at least that was the rumour."

I'm all at sea with this, but I need to understand. "How could it be that they were taken away when they had other family next door?"

"Their grandparents died a couple years earlier in a car accident," Ellie continues. "They had only the one child, Rosalie. She was your grandmother and my aunt. She'd become a drug addict, and she fell pregnant and had Jane, and then a couple of years later fell pregnant again and had Rachel. Neither of them had any known father. The grandparents cared for the girls and their daughter, Rosalie.

"After her parents died, Rosalie inherited the house, though she barely minded it. She moved a partner in, a violent man it was said, so perhaps it was him the welfare people were worried about.

There certainly was a lot of screaming between Rosalie and her fella. I think the neighbour on the other side complained of how Jane and Rachel were being abused. It was said, that after a court case, the children were adopted and the man was sent to jail, but I don't know any details.

Soon after they were taken away, Rosalie died. I heard rumours of suicide and a drug overdose, but I was too young to know what really happened. I've always held a hope that a kind family took them in and gave them a good life."

The gears are whirling in my mind and must be doing the same in Ellie's. She says, "That means your mother is my cousin Rachel. That makes me your aunt, and you and my children are second cousins.

"I actually went and sold you a house that belonged to our family. I should have given it to you! It was yours by birthright as much as mine. Maybe it stayed there waiting for you to come back into our family until the time was right for you to have it."

I hear a noise and look behind me. Marti has come up behind us as we're speaking. She looks in wonder from her mother to me, then walks over and hugs me. "Welcome to our family."

Later that evening, we make plans over an impromptu dinner that Kate and Marti, instant friends through blood, have whipped up.

There are now two things I must do.

Firstly, Kate and I must finish the exploration of my house, and I must show Kate and my new family the papers and gold I found hidden away there. It's likely they hold a story of how the house was built and came into our family.

The second and most urgent thing I must do is to return to the place of my birth, find those who knew my mother, and see what, if any, knowledge they hold. It's over thirty-seven years since I walked out of the door. I live in fading hope that somebody has kept her things, at least the small case of papers and her scrapbook. If I can find them, they may hide lost answers.

I don't know why this feels suddenly urgent, but it does. The numbers say friends of my mother are at least in their seventies by now, maybe older. Their health or memory could be failing. If they die, anything from my mother is unlikely to be passed on to a new generation.

With this new urgency in mind, before the night is done, Ellie and I have made a plan to travel to my hometown and see what fragments of my mother's past we can recover.

We'll fly to Armidale, rent a car, and drive out past Moree to my tiny home town, a place that barely shows on the map.

Chapter 28 – Jim – Place of my Birth

It's strange to return to a place you haven't seen in almost forty years when the place holds your entire childhood.

It's on the Gwydir Highway halfway from Moree to Collarenebri, about one hundred kilometres from each. It boasts a population of about 250 people, has its own public school, community hall and other minor facilities. These days it has gone slightly upmarket; it has its own café with an exotic sounding menu.

Everywhere is dry and dusty. It looks like little rain has fallen here in the last year, and green grass is barely in evidence, with only little remnants in local parks and people's yards. The season is moving from late spring towards summer, but it's already hot, with the bitumen blasting back heat as we drive up the main street. I wonder if there's water in the nearby river where we used to swim as kids in the summer. It always went dry in hot summers apart from a few stagnant pools, so I doubt people are swimming there now.

Why would my mother choose this Godforsaken place? But perhaps she didn't really choose and just took whatever job was on offer when she needed to leave her last one. Small and desolate though this town is, it did care for both her and me, taking us in and making us a part of their world.

I think it's become even more hollowed out since I lived here. It seems to me it's dying the same death as thousands of other small country towns, in which work and prosperity have shrunk away as people have moved to bigger towns and left local businesses to slowly die a lingering death.

I can instantly see why my mother wanted me to leave. Job or life prospects for a sixteen-year-old here are minimal.

After a brief look around the town, Ellie and I go to the local café for a late lunch. Maybe we'll pick up some local news and gossip there. The café is surprisingly full, with at least a dozen customers.

I'm interested in finding any old timers still living here, those who've continued on in this place on through the four decades from the time of my mother. Most patrons are young workers buying a late lunch. I see a couple old timers sitting at a table in a corner, women with the sun scarred look of hardy bush veterans.

We place an order. The waitress is young, friendly and definitely not from around here, with a European sounding accent, so I doubt she'll know much of the past. There's no sign of any owners, perhaps they're out back in the kitchen. Ellie and I have a quick chat about the best approach. We decide to try talking to the old timers in the corner.

Ellie is somewhere around their age with a friendly smile, so she volunteers to make the opening gambit. She wanders over and says, "Hello, I'm Ellie. I wonder if you can help me. I'm trying to find out about people in the town from way back. Can either of you tell me who would best know?"

She strikes instant gold. The women are long-standing friends from adjoining farms only a few miles away, and both are grandmothers. They treat themselves to lunch and gossip here each month. Today is our lucky day. One has lived here for thirty years since they bought a farm on the river, back when it had a good water allocation. It grows a range of crops on rich black soil, things like sunflower, canola and sorghum. The other woman has lived here all her life, being born and raised on a local sheep farm. Perhaps I even worked there as a lad, though any recollection I have of the farm's name is long gone.

They invite us to sit with them, and we make a table of four as they linger over deserts and cups of tea. For over an hour, they unpack the town's history in bite size chunks and, as expected, tell us a tale of its slow decline and neglect.

They don't remember my mother, but they do know the business owners who she did most of her work for. Their shop closed over twenty years ago, and the husband and wife who owned it both passed a couple years ago, but their daughter married a local farmer and still lives nearby.

I try to find out who else in town dates back to the time of my mother, and here I get another gem. There's an old bloke who lives a few hundred yards away, and he's been here forever. When we finish our meal, they offer to walk to his house with us and introduce us to him. "He has a sweet tooth, so you should buy one of the café's cakes to offer as afternoon tea if you want to get him to talk."

We arrive at his house at about 3.30 pm, which seems like a good time for a fresh cup of tea. Age has not been kind to the man who opens the door, with his craggy battle scarred features, but there's a buried familiarity in his features that I can't quite place.

He hasn't seen me since I was fifteen, but he knows me straight away. "Well, I'll be damned. How long has it been since you were a teenage rouse-about in my shed, reckon forty years near enough. How are you, James? You're looking better than me, that's for sure."

It's his voice that brings my memory back. This man ran a contract shearing team, based here, that covered a lot of stations across the north-west, from Moree to Lightning Ridge, up north to Mungundi, down to Narrabri and out to Walgett. I never went too far from home but, in school holidays, or at other times when he was short a man, he'd put me on wages in his shed. That must have begun when I was around twelve and continued until I left town. He was keen to get me working with a pair of shears and said I could soon become one of his gun shearers, but mostly my jobs were little things like crutching fly blown sheep.

His name is Tommy Haas, and I recall him telling people he was a half German mongrel, and a half Scots miser by descent. But he was a decent man who treated me fair. He was on the road much of his life but would call to see me and my mother when he was in town. I think he was a bit sweet on her, though she never gave him encouragement. But he was always keen to give me work. She trusted him to be honestr and keep me safe when I was in the sheds. He was almost like an uncle to me.

We sit and talk with Tommy until the light is fading. Ellie's input is small, but I can see her taking it all in. Eventually though, I see Ellie start to flag. It's been a long day for her. We make our apologies and I tell Tommy we'll see him tomorrow. He's offered to take us around the town and introduce us to people who knew my mother back then.

He only came to town when I was five and so doesn't know about my parentage. Nor does he know what happened to Mum's things, as he was away when she died. "Know people who should though. I'll do my best to help find answers. It's good to feel like I have a real job again."

Little by little, over the three days that follow, we put together what we can find out. One of the people Tommy introduces us to is Eileen, the first person to give my mother a job when she came to the town.

Eileen is now ninety but still sharp. "Well, I remember wanting to help her because she was pregnant when she came to town, and I knew she didn't have anyone else here. She'd come from a job as a domestic help and governess on some well-to-do property fifteen miles north of town. She worked there for two years after moving from a similar situation on a property between Moree and Warialda. She'd been there for a year, but she had to leave because their older son had wandering hands and would come in unannounced and try to trap her in rooms where she was working and force himself on her. Horrid man.

"She never told me much about the situation at the second property, other than to say she'd got pregnant one night when she let a shearer working on the property have his way. When she told him about you a couple months later, he denied you were his.

"I'm not so sure of that story, if I'm honest. There was also a rumour that the second son on the property, a man in his mid-twenties and engaged to the daughter of a nearby property, had got very fond of her. The two of them were seen together a good few times. However he was under pressure from his family to marry into another property without a son, to get his own place. And that's what he did.

"That's why some had an opinion she was carrying his child and, when he had spurned her on account of his own advancement, she came to town in need of employment, but determined not to tell anyone the truth.

It was said that, if his parents had known, they would have sought to raise you themselves, maybe adopting you and depriving your mother of you on the grounds of her promiscuity.

"Me, I think that's why she blamed her pregnancy on a sheep shearer to avoid them making an attempt to take you away. She may have been angry with men and the world at large because of what happened, but she loved you and would have done anything to protect you."

We meet several other townspeople who remember Mum, and they add in odd little bits, places where she worked, people who were her better friends, those she found time to say hello to or talk to. One person remembers her garden and how she once won a prize for her flowers in the local show, of which she was very proud.

One of the things I want most is to find out what happened to my mother's things, but the landlord of the house we rented and his wife both passed more than a decade ago, and nobody knows what they did with her possessions. It's presumed her clothes were donated to charity, and her furniture stayed in the house and was used by the next tenants.

As for my mother's other personal effects, her papers, nobody believes they would have been thrown out. "It would have been disrespectful," one old lady says, but nobody has any further information about where they may have gone.

As part of the town's slow decline, the house where we lived has been abandoned for a decade since the last tenants took work in Moree. The coat of paint I applied four decades past is still there, though now sunburnt, chipped and peeling back to bare weatherboards in many places. The fence and path are still the same, though all evidence of my mother's garden is gone. Now all that grows in the yard is a tangle of weeds, a few oleander shrubs and one stunted bougainvillea that a more recent tenant must have planted along the back fence. These shrubs all look half desiccated and in need of care and trimming.

The house is closed up but not securely. A few minutes of fiddling gets a window open. I climb inside and let Ellie and Tommy in through the front door.

There's nothing to show of our life back then, no remnants, but the bare walls and timber floors have carried through from our time. It looks like the last person to put a coat of paint on the inside was also me. I recognise the faded lilac colour of the walls, a colour my mother and I chose on a shopping visit to Moree. There's no furniture except for cupboards backing the kitchen sink, and these are empty. All the pieces of furniture my mother accumulated are gone, along with any signs of her personal touches or other effects.

I go outside and walk around the back. At last I see one familiar thing. It's a broken chair in a corner of the veranda. Its cushions are torn and one leg is broken. It was my mother's comfortable chair in her last months of declining health, a gift from a neighbour to give her a comfortable place to sit, from where she could look out over her garden when she was too frail to walk around and tend to it anymore. I would carry her in and out from the seat in those last weeks, and she would reward me with a small smile of gratitude, which was all she could manage. The memory brings me close to tears.

Ellie must notice my welling emotions, as she puts her hand on my arm as I show her and Tommy the chair and recount my memories of the garden and the chair to them in a half-choked voice. I can see tears in the corners of their eyes too as I speak of these final times in my mother's life.

"I remember her sitting there too the last time I visited," Tommy says. "I was away when she died, didn't get back until months later when new people were living here, so I never came back here again. Would you mind if I take the chair and fix it up? I'd like to have it to remember her by."

I smile and nod, and Ellie puts her hand on his arm in a show of support.

We load the chair into Tommy's utility, and then follow him on a tour of the rest of the town. There's not much to see. My ongoing feeling remains it's suffering the same malaise of decay as many other small country towns, not sudden death, but relentless terminal decline, not unlike my mother's path to the end.

That afternoon we say goodbye to Tommy for what I think is the last time. He promises to take a photo of the repaired chair and send it to me when he's done. He also says he'll also ask around about where the last tenants went in case they inherited any of my mother's things. "If I track down anyone else who may know what became of her things, you'll be the first to know."

Our final visit in the town is to the small graveyard. Strangely, my mother's grave is one of those better cared for. Tommy's work, I'll bet.

A simple headstone, which I'd long forgotten, lists the dates of her birth and death followed by the words:

Rachel Martin
Kind Friend to Many
Gracious to the End

Tommy's final words before we say goodbye to him give me a lump in my throat.

"Your mother was so brave and beautiful. I'd have married her in a flash if she'd have had me. But some thing or things had broken her trust in the world of men. I could never get past that.

"I'm really glad you've come back to try and put her memory to rights, Jim."

Chapter 29 – Kate – Uncovering Treasures

It's hard to imagine what new, unknown discoveries are yet to come into my life this year. So many wonderful things have already happened. I still have my Mum and Dad, and I love them as dearly as ever, and I now also have Jim. It's been such a happy time getting to know him and being able to talk to him with an open honesty I've never quite had with my parents.

But it's the connections that have come through Jim that most make my family feel complete. I've always been an only child. Although I have two uncles, an aunt and two cousins, I never saw much of them growing up, so mostly it's been just me and Mum and Dad.

Suddenly the circle has expanded. I now have a dozen cousins, five aunts and uncles in Brisbane, and a similar number in Sydney. I've met lots of them in short intense bursts over family dinners, but the one who has become my true friend is Marti. She's five years older than me but looks about my age. She's the youngest of Ellie's five children, the one who stayed home with her mother. Not that she doesn't get out. She has lots of friends and a very active social life.

But, like me, she's never met that special someone, and, like me, she's still living at home in her thirties but is happy and takes joy in being so close to her mother. In Marti, I've found the older sister I always wanted, one to give me advice and do things with. I think she likes the younger sister freshness I bring into her life.

Today, I call to see her after work so we can discuss our plan that we like to call either the 'Ganging up on Jim' or 'Making Jim explore the old house'.

"We should go see him tonight," Marti suggests. "He'll be back from working in the lumber yard now, won't he?"

Jim works three days a week at a lumber yard in Rozelle. The place is full of recycled timber from old houses, and he helps people find and match missing floorboards, skirtings and architraves, the things they'll need to restore all the inner-city terraces that have become trendy to live in. Jim's good with his hands, and there's nothing more I love than to watch him work, taking damaged remnants, turning them into usable products that sell for two or three times the price of new timber. He's amazing.

I grab my car keys. "Yep, reckon he will. I'll drive."

We arrive to see him sitting on a stool behind his house, beer in hand, staring into smoky nothingness. There are fires out the back of Sydney, in the mountains somewhere, and they've covered the city in haze.

We find two more stools, take the proffered beers and sit to chat, each telling a story or two from our day. During a lull in the conversation, Marti takes the lead and says, "Well, Jim, it must be time to see what's buried underneath the house, don't you reckon?"

Jim seems to be considering. "But what if we find buried treasure? Won't the state take it, say it belongs to them, don't they say that all these historic objects are state property or something similar?"

I shake my head. "Nope, this house isn't listed as a state historic object, even though it should be. And evidence suggests that anything here is family property. It's been in the family for a very long time, as per Ellie's story, for at least a hundred years, maybe even longer if we can establish a connection to the original builders.

"So, you'd have to report any finds, record and remove things found in a proper archaeological manner, and keep them for posterity, but you'd be the legal owner of anything found. If the state wants to buy anything you find, they'd have to agree on a price with you, unless whatever you find is clearly the property of others. Lucky you though. Because I hold an archaeologist's qualification, I can investigate the property. Well, I can if you chose to engage me. Of course if you do that, I'll need to get the proper permits because I work for the government. I may even ask that they appoint a supervising heritage officer to make sure it's all done legally. But that doesn't change the fact that anything you find still belongs to you."

Jim seems happier but still not quite satisfied. I know from his evasive manner that he's already found something important. I'm bursting to know what.

"But what if I found something like a big pile of old gold coins? Bet they'd try to take those off me."

Marti zooms in like a bee to honey. "Jim, spit it out. What've you found?"

Jim looks from Marti to me and back again. "Promise, scouts honour, that you won't tell anyone, well, not unless you're sure it's ours to keep?"

Marti nods emphatically and holds up her hand. "Scouts honour, I promise."

They both stare at me, and I realise they're actually serious about an oath. I know they have me. Family wins. I nod and raise my hand too. "Scouts honour."

Jim seems satisfied. He leads us behind the outhouse and points at a pile of dirt and rubble. He indicates for us to start moving this out of the way.

We do and make a fresh pile a couple metres away. He takes up a spade and begins to dig. I can see the earth is freshly dug, as the spade goes in easily. After ten minutes, he has a hole two feet across and two feet deep. A canvas wrapped object is at the bottom, new, not old canvas. He lifts this out. It's clearly heavy and makes a dull chinking sound as he sets it on the ground.

He shakes the last of the dirt away and pulls open the canvas wrapping to reveal a wooden crate. Inside this sit multiple bags of heavy cloth, each a hand-width in size. He lifts one up and passes it to me. He passes a second bag to Marti. The weight is surprising.

Jim picks up a third bag and carries it over to the table. We follow, each carrying our own bag. He unties a drawstring and tips the contents out. Dozens of gold coins spill across the table.

"Holy fuck!" Marti says. "That's a lot of gold coins."

I can feel my mouth fall open in astonishment.

Jim is grinning, then we're all grinning and laughing.

"That's part of what I found in the basement," he says. "There's so much more besides, but I just took out the money until I decided what to do. I didn't want somebody else to find it. I reckon it's finders keepers."

Marti nods enthusiastically.

I shrug. I can't disagree.

"As this house belongs to our family, I say this belongs to our family too," he says. "By my calculation, this gold pile weighs over fifteen kilograms. When I looked gold up last month, its street value was about a million dollars."

We collect all the bags of coins and bring them inside to count them. Each has two to three hundred gold coins. They're a mixture of golden guineas and gold sovereigns. The guineas are of earlier make, and the sovereigns are from the early 1800s. The latest I can find was minted in

1828. Based on this, it seems a good guess that these bags have sat here since soon after then, perhaps about 1830.

There are eight bags with an average of about two hundred and fifty coins per bag, so we're looking at about two thousand gold coins.

Marti Googles the weight of a gold sovereign. It comes up as a quarter of an ounce, say sixty to a pound weight or one hundred and thirty to the kilogram.

Googling the current gold price says $65,000 a kilogram. Jim's million-dollar value isn't too wide of the mark.

This is certain to be huge news. I can imagine our names splashed over the front of news articles before we can blink, being mobbed by journalists shoving microphones in our faces, all clamouring for a story. And this is only the beginning. I wonder what else is down there. Likely interest in the find makes my hands shake with excitement and terror in equal measure.

Jim's right. Despite my previous confident words, this could easily get out of control. For now, this is a secret only the three of us should know. Until we plan what to do, it's best if it stays that way. There's no way I'll let what my father's find be put at risk by any self-seeking public officials. I speak out these thoughts as they form.

Jim and Marti are in full nodding agreement. This belongs to our family. We'll keep it that way, and to hell with any consequences. This find's ours. It'll stay ours.

To give ourselves time to think, we make a cup of tea. Each of us takes a couple Tim Tam biscuits, a guaranteed sugar chocolate fix and brain reviver.

As we sit there, sipping, Marti pulls out a notebook and pen and jots down the plan we make, point by point, eight numbers in all.

1. *Lock gold coins securely away in a bank safety deposit box*
2. *Get a permit to formally investigate and reopen the basement*
3. *Catalogue what's there and document it in a short report (my job)*
4. *Secure the site to prevent any other people getting in or out*
5. *Invite heritage experts and media to see selected items off site*
6. *Disclose the source only with a binding non-disclosure agreement*
7. *Site tour for media and experts only if no location details revealed*
8. *When the fuss dies down inform people about the gold found.*

We all agree it's a good plan, and we'll set about making it happen. The only other person we will tell for now is Ellie.

"I'll fill out the permit application tomorrow and nominate myself as the heritage archaeologist," I say. "Marti, I'll put you down as my research assistant. Your job will be to photograph and map the location of anything I find, while I compile my report.

Jim, you should go with Ellie to the bank tomorrow and open a safety deposit box for the gold. Only you and Ellie will be able to access it. I won't lodge my excavation application until it's safely locked away.

"As the principal investigator, I'll need to nominate a second person to supervise my work in the event anything significant is found, and I know just the person. He's my former PhD supervisor. He's got impeccable credentials and he's absolutely incorruptible.

"He'll take delight in telling public officials to get out of his face if they try to bully information out of him or harass him. I defy anyone to question his skill or integrity. We won't tell him about the gold though."

"God, no," Marti says.

"I'll have to make my family connection known and say that's why I've offered to do the work myself. And I still have the notes from my first visit when I was called out as a Heritage Officer."

Marti looks between us all and smiles. "It'll make quite the story how you found your family because of that visit."

"Won't it just," Jim says.

"The important thing is that the details of the permit are protected by the Government Privacy Legislation. That means nobody's can disclose any information without your consent, Jim. It will allow us to manage this very tightly until we know what's down there and decide if we want to share that story with any journalists who're interested. No one will be able to badger or harass you or Ellie to find out. I'll make sure of that."

I lodge the permit form the next day and advise my boss in summary form of what I've found. I don't tell him much more than the basics set out in the application, and then I tell him I want to ask my professor to supervise the dig, so there'll be no question about it being done properly.

I trust my boss completely, so I hope in time I can tell him more than I am saying just now. I do tell him about the rediscovery of my father though.

"That's incredible! What are the odds. I couldn't be happier for you. That's a real feel-good story."

He barely raises an eyebrow when I explain that this is what caused the original investigation to be delayed, but now I've got to know my father and he trusts me, we want to go ahead, to learn about the house's history.

The application is approved by the Heritage Office within an hour. Later that afternoon I visit the professor who readily gives his agreement. He'll meet us on site on the following Monday, which is when we expect to be ready to start work.

To whet his appetite, I show him photos of the stonemason marks and give him the background about our finding the layer of stones beneath the floor.

"That's when my father called me. By the time I went on site, he'd already lifted a couple stones and found the stairs, but he stopped at that point when a friend at the pub told him he'd need a heritage permit.

I think the idea of breaking the law gave him cold feet, because he relaid the floor. He was worried the government would take his house off him.

"It's taken a bit of talking him around, but he trusts me, so he's agreed for the work to continue if I do it myself. He insisted on somebody outside of government supervising the digging because I still think he doesn't quite trust it. So I'm really grateful you've agreed to help us."

I can see Professor Small readily believes this story, which is at least partly true. I know he has little love for public officials himself. He's seen it too many times when the glory seekers leak details of excavations, no matter what promises they make in advance.

Chapter 30 – Marti – Story of a Basement

The job I'm going to be helping Kate with is so fascinating I've taken a week off work to help her.

I work as bookkeeper and office manager for a small engineering and construction firm, keeping track of the comings and goings of staff, organising computers and equipment and paying bills. Some of the skills I use at work will very much be the skills I'll use today, as we explore this reputed basement, as my main job will be to keep a log of who does what and when. I'll assign numbers to any objects found and record their precise locations. Then I'll photograph the items and label the photos with their item numbers. I'm also in charge of ordering food, equipment, and anything else we need, as the job progresses.

Kate and Jim have each put up $5000 to cover any expenses. My mother and I are happy to put in more money, if needed, to support this family project.

There's excitement in the air, a sense of incipient discovery that I feel thrilled to be a part of.

The others on site are Professor Small, Kate, her mum and dad, Ellie, Jim, and one of his lumber yard mates. Jim and his friend will be the diggers who'll remove the dirt and stones and store them for return later, as well as do any other hard manual labour. Jim's mate will be paid a day rate as a worker, while the rest of us are doing it for love.

Kate wanted to pay Professor Small a fee, but he refused. He's says he's happy to do it for the excitement of the hunt, but if Kate makes any significant finds, she can donate an item to his collection of Australian colonial artefacts that he uses to educate his university class. It all sounds fair to me.

We gather in the back room of the house. It's empty except for a table and chair for me to work at, a laptop that's running a spreadsheet to keep track of anything we find, and a paper log book where every find or action will be logged with its time, a short description and a number, which will be cross checked against the spreadsheet regularly.

Kate gives us a short description of what's known of the history of the house and how it came into her father's hands. She outlines today's work and stresses this could be a highly significant site, based on what's been found to date, such as old builder marks. So it's important there be no pub talk or other information getting out until we've finished and are ready to announce any finds.

The professor takes over and gives a short talk about the importance of provenance in these investigations; that means we need to know and record the exact location of everything found, whether removed or left in place.

He says, "We must do that to provide this information for posterity. It's my job is to ensure this is done completely and accurately."

We get to work. It only takes two hours to take up the re-laid paving stones, photograph each of them, map their original positions, and stack them out back. After that, Jim and his mate remove the underfloor layer of clean sand, which lets us get a good look at the pattern of the original square stones sitting below the old floor. Despite being told what to expect, there's something about seeing the real thing that alights my imagination.

Kate points out two early mason marks on stones and shows us a picture from a matching stone at the Conservatorium of Music. "This mark was linked to an

1820s group of stone masons called 'The Irish Brothers'. Very little is known about them, but what we do know is that their marks are found on several important Sydney buildings that date to around the 1820s."

Jim lifts the first stone and then its next door mate to reveal the descending set of stairs.

We all draw in our breath at this sight that's been hidden for perhaps one hundred and eighty years.

"This is as far as I got last time," Jim says. "On the advice of a friend I called the Heritage Office at that point, as I realised it may be an important historic site."

Not quite true, but we want to establish another slightly changed history that will become the officially recorded version. I duly note it in my log book to give the statement a documented authenticity.

Now Jim and his mate carefully scrape away the old mortar which holds the adjoining stones in place. In half an hour, another four square stones have been lifted clear, giving full access to the stairs.

Kate passes a torch to Professor Small and invites him to lead the way. She follows him down the stairs while the rest of us stand back.

As he reaches the bottom, his footfalls cease, and we hear a low whistle. "My God, this is amazing. There are enough bottles here to get a whole army drunk."

We wait in anticipation for something more substantial. For a while, all we hear is the sound of odd shuffling footsteps and grunts of interest. Then, at last, we hear them coming back up the stairs.

"Well?" we all ask in unison.

Kate is grinning from ear to ear. The prof's expression is more restrained, but he's very excited too.

"A veritable treasure trove," he says. "There's a gold mine of information buried down there. We've only had a preliminary look, but we suspect it's an illegal still that operated in the 1820s and maybe the 1830s. There are hundreds of bottles of liquor, unopened bottles, and an abundance of papers and other early material.

"It'll have to be carefully analysed, of course, I'd say it'll be a work of several weeks at least. But I think I can honestly say this is one of the most significant finds in the early colonial history of Sydney.

"It appears to have stayed sealed up for a very long time. A page of an old letter gives us a clue as to why. The letter is dated in the early 1830s, sent from Ireland, asking for their son Michael to come home and help with the family farm in County Cork. It may be that he sealed up his liquor business and went home, expecting to return, but never made it back."

Professor Small turns to Jim. "We're going to need help with this one. It's way too big for Kate to do it alone. I want to put on a least three or four students to work on it, as a research project over six months. That way we can carefully catalogue and record everything. It will all be left in place, but this is far too important to keep hidden away.

"I know it's your family's past, but it's also a vital part of the story of very early Australian colonial history, so I seek your agreement to do it properly. We'll keep it quiet, but we need to reveal a few details to keep it safe from even more prying eyes. If we do it this way, I think I can get both the NSW Government and the university to each pay their share in the cost of conserving this national treasure."

I wonder how Jim will react. He looks surprisingly relaxed, almost like he expected something like this. Perhaps he's realised much bigger things are at play here than just family secrets.

He nods. "That sounds reasonable, but I do want Kate and I to work here throughout, and I want us to get the first chance to read the documents down there. If you like, you can make a copy for us and keep the originals safe, but I want to know whatever this tells me about our family before it finds its way onto the front pages of the newspapers.

"And, if I'm going to lose use of my house for months, somebody's going to have to pay for another place for me to live until the work's finished. Kate will also need a wage if she's doing this instead of her regular work, and, of course, the site must be made fully secure, so no louts or vandals can break in. Make all that happen and you have a deal."

The Prof screws up his face, although it's all entirely reasonable and hard to argue with. I sense Jim has grown another foot in Professor Small's eyes for his shrewdness as he lays out his demands.

"Well, Jim, I see you drive a hard bargain, but I can't argue with your demands. They're what I would have asked for if I was in your shoes, except I would have asked for a wage for myself too, seeing as you'll be working full time here and not able to work elsewhere. So, why don't you add that to your list.

"As for Kate, I'll tell the head of the Heritage mob that her services are required here and this is more important for now. They can keep paying her wage until the work's finished. Does that sound fair?"

Jim surprises me when he says, "Thanks for the offer to pay me Prof but, if it's all the same, I'll meet my own keep. If I need money I can flog off a few of those bottles below to collectors. I reckon they'd pay a good penny for a bottle of a first edition drop from one of the Irish Brothers."

The Prof raises an eyebrow. "Considering you've never been below that's most interesting knowledge you have. But then you never made those footstep marks in the dust of the stairs now, did you?

Jim grins. "Well, that's one for you, Prof." He doffs the hat he's wearing, a mischievous glint in his eye.

With that, the deal is done.

I look at Jim with admiration. I suspected he was smart, despite his often shabby appearance but, in that moment, I've seen a man of much greater stature.

Jim must have been impressive in his younger days. He's about six foot two with the spare athletic build of an Australian Rules player, albeit softened with age. There's also a look about him that's dark and fierce, despite the silver tips in his hair.

As I try to place it in my mind, I decide it's part a look of a Viking warrior but with a dash of something between Italian and aboriginal in his dark hair and strong features. It's easy to see how the ladies loved him in his youth. Even now, the virility is still there.

Kate's adoptive parents are impressive too, but in a more urbane and polished way. This man has something untamed that inspires me. I'm glad he's become part of my family.

In that moment, I have an inspiration. The family once owned the house next door. It was the house of Jim's grandmother and great grandparents, the place where his mother was born. It seems fitting that somehow the house should be returned to Jim and Kate.

Perhaps the gold Jim has found could be the solution, though that might take time to sort out. We'd have to find a way to either delay the sale, or temporarily find money from elsewhere.

I'd really love to have Kate, who feels like a younger sister, living next door. Making it happen may also be part recompense for an awful past in this family branch.

Chapter 31 – Mick – The Returning-1832

The boat has just pulled into Cork Harbour, my first sight of Ireland since I was seventeen, over thirteen years ago. It was wonderful to see and smell those green mist covered hills as we sailed past a bluff that a sailor told me is Roches Point, with the nearby town of Cobh, then up the River Lee to the Cork docks.

As we tie up and I look about, I find I have tears in my eyes at being back in the land of my birth, a place I never thought I'd see again.

A fair lot of people get off and many new ones line up to come on board. I go ashore and buy a feast of bacon and cabbage, a meal my mother served at times of extra money, like after we sold a fat pig. It tastes so good. With it a flood of memories of my home come pouring into my mind, on top of the sights and smells of those hills.

I was never in Cork Town before; it's several day's walk from my home near Schull, but it's a bustling port full of buyers, sellers and wheeler-dealers. This day the musical tongue of Cork people, along with those other familiar sights and sounds, is almost overwhelming. At the same time, it gives me comfort of a sort I have not experienced in more years than I can bring to mind, a feeling of a lost childhood. So, for a while, I sit and stare, drinking it all in, until it becomes dark in the short evening twilight. Cold bites into my softened skin as I reboard the boat for my final leg home.

I awake in the early dawn to a solid sea swell rocking me about. From the deck, I spy rolling breakers pounding into the beetling cliffs of the coast a few miles away. A day of slow sailing follows, pounding through a heavy swell, passing landmarks such as Old Head and then

Seven Heads that the captain calls out before dark falls again. In the night, we see, in the northern distance, the towering light of Galley Head Lighthouse, and, in the early dawn, the Clear Island light comes into view.

This boat sailed from Portsmouth, at the bottom of England, the place from which I was first transported. It's bound for the new lands of America, heading across to a place called Boston. Its human cargo is a mixed load of Irish and English free settlers, seeking a new home in a land of opportunity, along with a few like me making a short journey to Erin. It's crowded but friendly. Jokes and laughter make the journey feel light.

Our final stop is Crookhaven Harbour, near the south-west tip of Ireland, from where I will alight. I know it's a twenty mile walk from the harbour to our house in the rocky hills rising up behind the town of Schull, the place where our farm lies. I remember our farm as a barren rocky place that looks out over fertile lands in the valley below. I could walk from here in a day if I need to, but I have hope of hiring a man with a sound horse and cart, even a grand carriage, so as to bring me home in an easier manner.

I've gotten accustomed to comfort in my Sydney colonial life, where I own a fine buggy with two strong horses to draw it. As a result, I've grown softer in my physical stamina in the last half decade. Plus, I've a good pile of luggage to bring along, things I must otherwise leave in the port, to collect later, if no horse drawn carriage is to be found.

We arrive into Crookhaven in the mid-morning. I look in amazement at this prosperous port. I've never been here, but I hear it's grown in size in the last century. It's used as a final stopping point for boats making the trip across to the New World. Here they replenish stores of food and water for the hazardous trip west into the wild open ocean.

It's a great Irish harbour, one wonderfully protected by a spit of land to its seaward side, which blocks the rolling breakers and gales. The port is two miles long by up to a half mile wide. On this day it's so crowded with ships one could almost walk from deck to deck across the harbour, as they sit moored in great profusion.

There's no space to dock. As I'm the only departing passenger, the ship's captain hails a row boat which comes alongside. A crewman lowers me and my things into it, at the same time giving instructions for more food and water to be brought on board before they sail on. There are two new crew to come aboard here. They will come out on the next trip of the rowboat.

I wave goodbye to my newfound friends, and they wish me well in my homecoming, for which I felt a new trepidation. It's noon when I disembark, and there are no carts to be had until the morrow, so I take a jar of ale and pay for a night's lodging in one of the many ale houses that line the harbour. In truth, I'm happy to have a night with my feet standing on solid ground before I make the final leg of my long journey.

I find myself in awe of the industry of this place. In the falling dusk, I walk along the harbour getting a feel for it. It's clearly a booming business hub and ships pay premium prices for provisions they take on here. I've developed a sharp business mind in the last decade and see much profit is made in this place. Fresh food and vegetables are most valuable as the land around here is poor, meaning little local produce of quality is available.

By contrast, the farm lands in the valley below our farm are rich and fertile. Any produce grown there would command a premium price here. While there's already some business of that nature here, it seems but little, with most merchants bringing in produce from much further afield.

As I walk the port-side streets, I talk to several people who have travelled for multiple days with loaded carts to reach this place. They tell me what produce is in most demand and prices paid. It's good food for thought should I end up staying here longer than I plan.

The next day, I depart early, having paid a nominal sum for a hauler to bring me and my goods to my local town as back-loading in his empty cart. It's a slow journey, as his great draft horse walks at a steady pace along the return leg, pulling a large, near empty, four-wheel wagon. He's heading up into the midlands of Cork, where he will have his cart replenished for the shipping trade.

My things only take up a small corner, but the hauler is glad of the extra business I give him, money he can keep, unknown to his boss.

He's a dour character, little given to conversation. I alternate between walking beside the cart, sitting in it, and, at times, taking small detours into the nearby countryside to enjoy its sights and sounds. From these jaunts I can easily catch up with the man, his cart and his heavy horse.

It's late in the day before we reach Schull, the town where he plans to stop for the night. He will give his horse a spell in a stable at the end of town while he uses my fare to pay for a night of drink at a local tavern.

It seems a fair exchange to me. As a bonus to him for arranging to have my gear stacked in a back corner of the stable until I return for it, I buy him his first pint and a plate of food before I set out on the two mile walk up into dark looming hills, half seen in the fading evening light.

I'm now anxious to be home to see my father and brother. I hope that my mother lives yet as well. It seems in another life when I saw them last.

It takes a bare half hour of brisk walking until I spy their stone house on a rise a half mile ahead in the dim light. There is smoke rising from the chimney and, again, I feel tears in my eyes at this familiar sight.

I shout out and bang on the door until my father, looking much aged and diminished, opens it to me. It takes long seconds until he knows me, but his delight on my recognition is so strong he can barely stand. He brings me in. I see how diminished my mother and brother are, but at least they live yet. In the town, knowing they may have little to eat, I bought a fresh loaf of bread and a good piece of cheese and ham which I put on the table. We settle in to share all our stories of the decade past.

It's a simple homecoming, and I'm glad to be home.

I have forgotten just how poor is the land on our farm. The most part is rock. A dozen sheep pick a half living, eating grass scattered amongst gorse and heather.

There are a few areas where enough stone is piled up to leave the fields half clear and make space to pasture a cow and horse. There's an area set aside for a fair crop of potatoes, but this area is small, and the soil's not deep enough for them to grow fully big and fat.

As I look back, I think it's no wonder I took to petty crime. There was not enough of a living for a family of five to survive on this plot. We all needed to do odd jobs, off farm, to fill our bellies, and with time on our hands between jobs, trouble was sure to follow.

I feel most sorry for my brother, Neil. He was getting the farm into good production when the accident happened. He was even engaged to a girl down the road, and with extra land from her side, there was promise of a fair living for them both and for the children expected to follow.

Now she's abandoned him.

I don't blame her; it was too hard to throw her life away as a young woman and marry a cripple. She walked away from the engagement and found another man, leaving my little brother very low.

He is still a good lad with a good brain. But all he does is sit in a chair by the fire the whole day, staring moodily around, letting the world drift by.

It's no sort of life for him. He needs a good shaking. But neither my father nor mother has enough fire left in them to change this. So I reckon it's up to me to wake him up again.

After a week, I've bought a new cart and a fine young horse to pull it, and I've put the word out about wanting to buy good fields on the valley flat.

I've brought one of my bags of gold coins with me. A small part of this will buy good farmland down there, maybe ten or twenty acres. It would be best if we could buy land with a cottage on it, to save us having to go up and down the hill. That way we can keep these hill lands for sheep and live below on the good land. Down there we can grow produce to supply the ships.

I'm sure a chance will come to buy this soon.

If not, once I get the right bit of land, I will build a house for our family on it. It would be best built up the back where the first hills begin, a place with a fine view but only a short step to the farmlands we work on.

My brother has caught my enthusiasm. I always knew he was smart. Now he has something to do, besides sit and think, his mind has come back alive again. He spends hours each day talking with me about all the details of our plans to supply ships coming to Crookhaven Harbour and headed for America, such things as what to grow, how to transport it, whether to get a small boat to take it from Schull rather than haul it overland. Much of this detail I've not thought of. I find it's exciting to work on this together.

It is good to have him active again. He's much better for it and is often the first to rise in the morning these days. His bed is against the wall, alongside the fireplace. Before he just lay there waiting for another to rise and rebuild the fire, now it's his first task of the morning. He has still got good use of his arms and shoulders though his legs can do little. So, he's able to pull himself around and do things, but he'd grown lazy, feeling sorry for himself, leaving it all to my mother.

Not having to care for him and work the farm has given my mother and father a new lease of life, for which I'm doubly thankful. I think they both have more years left in them than I'd thought before.

As for my brother, he's determined to do more things on the farm as well as to plan. To help him get around, I've found two good sticks to use as crutches. His arms are well able to carry him this way, though his legs barely work.

With the sticks, he can lift himself and half walk on flat ground. Thus, going steadily along, he can pull himself around the farm, even lift himself onto the cart seat and use his arms to drive around, doing things like taking loads of goods into town and getting out to meet old friends at the market, as well as doing simple tasks on the farm.

And the great news is we've found ten acres of fine flat land for lease below with a small cottage alongside.

It's ideal and, if the land does produce as expected, I am sure we can reach agreement on its purchase plus more nearby besides. My brother's keen and I'm keen. All it needs is a little luck and some good hard work.

Part of me feels a great yen to return to my family in Sydney. Over six months have passed since I said goodbye and I would dearly love to see their small brown faces again. But I cannot leave now. I am just getting things on their feet.

Soon it will be Christmas. Perhaps, by Easter, I'll have got things here running well enough to return to my other place over the sea. But another part of me wants to see this venture through to real success. It's too cold to grow much now but, after Easter, it should be right to plant crops and sell a fine load of the county's best food to provision those ships. Perhaps I'll stay on until the autumn when the produce is all harvested and sold.

I'm sure it will return a tidy profit. I intend to give each family member a quarter share. It seems only fair.

Chapter 32 – Kate – Michael O'Flaherty?

Professor Small has assigned me four students to assist with a systematic survey of Jim's house and its original contents, as discussed and agreed. One is surveying the external structures of the house and yard, documenting and recording everything that's there, each stone and mark, each other structure such as outbuildings, walls, porches, roof supports and chimneys.

The second student is recording the early internal structures: walls, floors, doors, plumbing, window mounts and fireplaces. The list goes on.

The other two students are working with me in the basement, doing a quadrant by quadrant inventory, first a detailed visual examination and photographic record of each section, then taking out the contents of each part to get individual item details, things like removing all the bottles on the racks, one by one, photographing the front and back of each, taking a weight record and other relevant information, before returning each to its original place.

It's Jim's property after all, so we must be extra careful to avoid damage to anything.

It's slow painstaking work, but it's essential if we want to know the exact position and condition of each item prior to disturbance and have an accurate record.

My main job is the oversight of it all, really just to cruise around, noting and looking at discoveries of interest, scanning papers found and ensuring no shortcuts are taken. It's going well. By the third day, we've documented all the major artefacts and are starting to go through the papers and other small items.

The papers are where my main interest lies.

After each has been logged and copied, I look at each document for important information. Many are receipts for sales made and records of deliveries. The volume supplied is substantial, with between fifty and one hundred bottles a week going to various buyers, most with no more identification than initials. The payments are equally vague. Most only list a number of guineas or sovereigns paid using initials for specific items. Much is in shorthand, things like 2 Ab, 3 Gi, 4 Wh to DP - 6 Sov. I presume this refers to the number of bottles of gin, whiskey and absinthe being supplied for a number of Gold Sovereigns. These spirits are the three main items with which the shelves are stocked. It's interesting that some bottles bear labels suggesting the whiskey's from Scotland, the gin from London and the absinthe from Paris, even though other evidence suggests most is produced or at least bottled here. There are labels on some bottles referencing the name Michael Kelly and a few indicating produce of the Irish Brothers, but most are unlabelled, so I suspect most labels are applied later by final sellers, allowing them to claim and use their own provenance information.

There are also innumerable papers that look as if they relate to other building or business ventures. These include sale records for garden produce, plans for building houses, information on supplies of stone and its cartage, and receipts for sales and purchases of building goods such as timber posts, red cedar for furniture, and built cabinets.

All these papers are of secondary interest. What I'm most looking for are personal letters, diaries or other records that can tell us something about these people and their lives. So far, these pickings are slim. It looks like whoever built this place must have kept private records in another place or, perhaps, they were taken with him when he left.

At last, at the bottom of a pile of papers, I find something interesting. It's an open envelope with no contents but with an address that seems to relate to this place. It's addressed to Michael O'Flaherty. I wonder if it matches the page of the letter Professor Small found on the first day, the request to return to Ireland.

The sender's address is on the back, a Father Terry Riley, Parish Priest of Schull, on behalf of Mr Joseph and Mrs Mary O'Flaherty of Hill Farm, Schull. It's dated Easter, 1827. It would have taken at least six months to reach him, so it's arrival was probably late in 1827 or early 1828. Other receipts and early coins show he lived here for at least three years after that. Perhaps it held another letter no longer here.

The rest of the papers reveal nothing of great importance, though the first names Mike and Mick appear in many places suggesting that the owner of this place was Michael O'Flaherty. While some bottle labels refer to a Michael Kelly, but I suspect this is just a ruse to keep the identity of the real owner hidden from view.

In all, we have fragments of a story, but the story is largely incomplete. We'll have to search back through the early title folios to get something more, though maybe there's another way.

Perhaps the town from which this letter came is a better place to start. It seems there was a correspondence between Michael O'Flaherty and a place in Ireland, which may have been his home. Perhaps somebody in Ireland will know about him, even if he lived almost two hundred years ago.

I've heard that parish records of births, deaths and marriages are a good source of family information and, as

I have the name of a parish priest from 1827 who wrote to Michael on behalf of his probable parents, this would seem the best place to start. His parents were most likely illiterate but are likely to have been born, married and died in the parish. I'll try to find out more from the records there.

It would be much easier if there wasn't a large time difference, and better still if I could visit in person. Even so, a couple hours spent on the phone in the middle of the night may yield something useful, or at least get me contact details of a person who currently works in the parish and who can access old records.

I'm about to commit to doing this when I think of Josephine. We've kept in touch by email, at least weekly, in the two months since she went away. She's recently been travelling in Europe and last week emailed from London. She told me she's spending a week there and then heading to Ireland where she'll hire a car to drive around the coast, staying in country pubs and castles, particularly along the south and west coasts.

My geography of Ireland's not strong, but I'm pretty sure Schull is in County Cork on Ireland's south coast.

Perhaps Josephine could visit Schull to see what she can find out by going direct to the original sources. If for no other purpose, emailing to ask her will be another excuse for us to stay in touch. This is something that Josephine also seems keen to do too.

I pull out my laptop and pen off a short email.

Jo,
As you know we're excavating Jim's house basement.
Interesting - lots of bottles of grog almost 200 years old. It still looks good. I wonder how it tastes.
But I'm struggling to find anything about the original owner.
It appears his name was Michael O'Flaherty and he came from the Parish of Schull in County Cork, to Australia.
I think his parents lived there in 1827.
We've found an empty envelope for what looks like a letter to him. It appears to have come from his parents but we think it was written by the Parish priest, a Terry Riley.
If you get the chance to go there, could you try and call into the local church and look up the parish records to see if we can find out about the family back then, details of their births, deaths, marriages or whatever exists from 1800 to 1850.

Lots of love and hope to see you again soon,
Kate

Chapter 33 – Josephine – Irish Connection

Yesterday, I got a delightful email from Kate. Each time I see a message from her, I smile and want to hug her. She's like the daughter I never had.

I'm slowly finding peace of mind after the overwhelming sense of guilt I felt before I left. When I stood beside Cindy's grave, my sense was I'd failed my best friend in her hour of greatest need, and it was traitorous to take her place in the centre of her family.

Kate certainly doesn't feel that way. She's told me I was her mother's true friend who did my best to help her, and it's not my fault things spun out of control that day. She said I was not to know what would happen, and she doesn't blame me in any way.

The thought of Jim tears at my heart every day. I'd wanted him to come after me and beg me to stay, to convince me he loved me for myself and not just as a pale substitute for his former wife.

I see now he could not do that. He's been too damaged by a lifetime of loss to expect better than what I did in leaving him. Each time a new bad thing happens, he just shoulders his fate and battles on, foot in front of foot, to get through each new day.

Knowing this, I see I need to make the next move, to return and give him myself to him without limit, to bring him joy, to make him smile and whistle again.

Is it hubris on my part to think I can do that for him? I dearly hope not.

I'm not quite ready to return just yet. I'm still finding bits of myself, but I think I'll be ready soon. And now, after reading Kate's email, I know I have a real job to do. I'm happy to change my planned route and be delayed for a day or two. I'm even happy to change flights if it means I can help Jim and Kate.

I'm glad to take up this task.

Last night, I checked into a small bed and breakfast in Schull. My host served me a cooked breakfast in the best Irish tradition: home cooked brown soda bread, bacon, egg, tomato, mushrooms and black pudding, and then gave me directions to the parish church, along with a suggestion I go to lunchtime mass, which is usually only attended by a handful of the elderly.

"The priest is bound to be grateful for any new parishioner, so he'll hardly refuse your request to look at the old parish records. I'm told they go back for over three hundred years. The priest is a bit slow and doddery these days, so it may take him a while to locate them all and show them to you. Take a cake with you from the shop in the middle of town. He's always one for a slice. You'll be able to look at the records over a cup of tea. You'll make his day."

I follow the directions, and I'm one of only three people present at mass. After the service, the priest, who says his name is Paddy Murphy, waits to shake my hand. "I hope you enjoyed the service. It's an absolute delight to meet you. I trust you'll join us again soon."

"Well, actually, Father Murphy, there's something I hope you can help me with, that's if you've time today." I tell him about my hope of checking the parish records. Having seen his tiny flock, I know he'll be hard pushed to refuse me.

He leads me to the vestry and opens a cupboard laden with heavy old books, at least twenty of them, covering all the shelves. He shakes his head and looks at them with dismay. "It might be a big job. I fear we'll both be here all day and night. I still have my evening mass to say."

I offer him an escape. "I have a cake which I hoped we might share. Why don't you make us both a pot of tea? I'll get to work looking through these, that's if you're are happy to let me. My eyes are a bit younger than yours, and you can get on with other things."

He nods, so I pass the cake over, and he gratefully toddles off. In ten minutes, he returns with a teapot and the cake on a plate, while I set to work.

It takes a while to sort the books into date order. First I go through them looking for the right time period. I begin with the register of births used in 1800, and check each entry, line by line. My first discovery comes soon. Connor O'Flaherty was baptised here in 1800, followed by his brother, Michael, a year later. Their sister Marie is mentioned two years later, then their brother Neil five years further on. In the best of biblical tradition, their parents are called Joseph and Mary, and the address is listed as Hill Farm, followed by a strange Irish name, Skeagh, which I've never heard of before. Perhaps it's a locality name. The priest's notation in the register is 'Father T Riley'. I'm glad this confirms there's a man named Michael O'Flaherty who grew up in this parish two hundred years ago, and that the parish priest back then was Father Riley.

I shoot off a quick email to Kate before I continue looking. Now I need to try and find out what happened to the next generation. It's reasonable that some of them, once grown, were married here and had children of their own, so I turn to the Marriage Register. Sure enough, in 1821, an eighteen-year-old Marie O'Flaherty married Dougal Mahoney. Dougal is from a town I drove through a few miles down the road towards Cork. After the marriage, I suspect records will show Marie Mahoney now lives in another parish where her children will be baptised. I flick through the Marriage Register for the rest of the decade, finding nothing, even though one might expect at least one of the three brothers to stay on the farm and marry.

I'm about to give up, having reached 1835, when another entry jumps out at me. Michael O'Flaherty marries Rosemary Roche. The listed address of the groom isn't Hill Farm but another farm near Schull. It's in a locality called Corthna. Rosemary Roche is listed as coming from Crookhaven, which I know from my trip planning is a major port twenty miles down the road, which, back then, was the last provisioning point for ships en route to America.

These are tantalising fragments of the life of a man supposed to be living in Sydney in the late 1820s. Perhaps he prospered in Sydney and returned to his homeland, where he bought another farm not far from his family home.

I pick up the Death Register to see if there's any information as to the fate of Michael's parents. I begin at the time when the youngest child was born, just in case the mother died at or soon after childbirth, which wasn't so unusual in those days. There's nothing listed, and it's not until I get to the 1820s that I find the next notation for the family. The eldest son, Connor, died from pleurisy at the age of twenty-six in 1826, a few years after his sister's marriage. I check through the next decade's worth of records, but there's no further information about any of these names.

I'll have to turn to other sources to try and find out what became of members of these families. Perhaps a local historian or librarian can help, perhaps the farms where these people once lived still exist and a family lineage continues which has retained parts of the story.

I show the priest what I've gathered and ask him about other ways to find out about these people. His explanation is rambling and convoluted.

"Well, you could try in Skibbereen, that's the first proper town near here with a library, but then again it's a bit far away. And then there's Mrs Major. She owns the shop at the edge of town. It's been in her family since time began. No gossip slips past her. In summer, farmers often stop there for a mineral or ice cream on the way to town. Then there's old Mary Mahoney. She knows a good bit. What did you say was the name of the one, the daughter that got married? All the Mahoneys round here are related, so she'll know of all the family going back, to be sure. She was from Ballydehob. It's a different parish, and maybe you could find more there. Then again, what did you say was the name of the farm they came from? Hill Farm, Skeagh? I know where it is right enough; tis desolate country up in the hills. Don't think you'll find anyone there. Most houses are sheep sheds these days."

When the ramble is finished, I'm little the wiser, but I think Mrs Major is a good place to start. I thank him profusely and get him to show me where to find her shop on my local map.

In ten minutes, I'm there enjoying one of her famous ice creams and a chat. As was expected, Eileen Major is a local goldmine of information, knowing at least a part of the story that I'm seeking.

It turns out the O'Flaherty's became a prosperous family around here. She knows about the younger brother, Neil, but little of Michael, though she has heard a couple of family members mention his name in passing, calling him great grand-uncle Michael, who went to America.

"Neil was something of a local legend," Eileen says. "He was crippled in a horse accident in his early twenties, so the story goes, breaking his back. But he taught himself to walk again after a fashion. He went from living on a poor rough hill farm up the back where the rocky hills rise, a place that would barely feed a sheep and a goat, to buying the best land around here, two hundred acres of fertile, flat farmland to supply the boats out of Crookhaven.

"It's said he would drive a dray round each day, check on all the workers, keeping them on their toes, but also have his cart loaded with many things they needed. At times, he would drive the dray down to Crookhaven despite his crippled state. And he raised a fine family of four girls and four boys, despite his impairment.

"They continued the place on when he died, until the late eighteen hundreds when, as often happens with the next generation, they started fighting amongst themselves.

Once the steamships took over, Crookhaven began to die. Boats no longer needed to stop off there for extra provisions, so the export business slowly dried up. In the end, all their farmland was sold off, and all that remained was the grand house he built. You can still see it to this day; it's four miles down the road towards Barley Cove. Look out to your right and you'll surely see it there. It's said to have cost five thousand pounds to build, a huge sum back then.

"The great, great, great granddaughter lives there to this day. Her name is Kathleen. If you call to see her and tell her I sent you with a packet of her favourite biscuits, I'm sure she'll share with you what she knows."

She takes a packet of Jaffa Cakes from the shelf.

I go to pay her, but she says, "No need. This one's on me. But call back later and tell me what you find out. I always love a good story."

Half an hour later, I'm sitting and having a cup of tea with Kathleen. She's an elderly lady who looks nearer to ninety than eighty, but her mind is still clear and, when the name of Michael O'Flaherty is spoken, she immediately knows who I'm talking about. In the space of a few minutes, she fills me in on the basic family story of his life. "The family story has been handed down over a good few generations, so I can't swear to its total accuracy, but I think it's mostly true, and the bits about Neil are definitely true.

"If you want to go right back, the original O'Flaherty family had a very poor farm in the hills behind the town." She points to a towering mountain, named Mount Gabriel, in a range which rises up to dominate our view, and indicates an approximate location on its northern slopes.

"Their farm was in a valley in those hills with poor rocky soil. It was good for sheep but not much else, so their life was hard, and they often lacked food in the house. Still, they survived in a limited but happy way. My great-great grandfather Neil was the youngest child, and he loved the farming life. It's said he followed his oldest brother, Connor, around the farm with a puppy dog like adoration.

"The second brother, Michael was a wild child. The story is he didn't have to be responsible in the way his older brother, who was expected to take over the farm, did. So, starting in his teenage years, he was often out with friends, getting into trouble. It all came to a head when he was seventeen and he and two others were caught stealing a pig from a rich farmer, a Protestant of English descent and sympathies. The other two were younger, both sixteen. They put the blame on Michael, said he encouraged them to do it, which was probably true. He was tried by the local magistrate and found guilty on the evidence of his friends.

"In those days stealing livestock was a hanging offence. But, as he was young and had never done it before, instead he was sentenced to transportation to Sydney for seven years. He was sent to England in chains and kept in a hulk in Portsmouth until he was shipped out.

"Michael was also the clever one though. Along the way, he'd learned to read and write, taught by the local priest, Father Riley, who had a soft spot for him. Michael served as an altar boy until his teenage years.

"Michael wrote Father Riley a letter each year to read to his family. They told of how he had made a successful life for himself in Sydney and that, once his convict term was done, he'd started a building business in the colony where the demand for new houses was high, and how he now owned ten acres of land in his own farm, which was making a good income selling produce to the colony.

"While he was in Sydney, his sister Marie got married to the son of a well-to-do landowner from ten miles down the road, near Ballydehob, meaning the farm only had to support four not six people. So, all was going well in both Ireland and Australia, until the older brother Connor died of pleurisy in the bad winter of 1826. Neil and the whole family were devastated at his death, but Neil, then eighteen, set about building up the farm following Connor's ideas. Over the next few years, he improved it until it produced more than enough for the family to live on. He was engaged to be married to a local girl and all was well until he had his accident.

He was driving the cart to town with a load of potatoes to sell, and the horse was startled by a badger in the ditch. It reared, capsizing the cart on top of him, breaking his back. He lost almost all use of his legs and gave up on life. His fiancé broke off the engagement, saying she didn't want to marry a cripple.

"After that, Neil just sit on a chair at home doing nothing while his ma and da, both getting old and tired, struggled on with caring for him and also running the farm. In desperation, his father went to see Father Riley. He asked him to write a letter to Michael, begging him to return home to help the family.

"A year or so later, Michael, now a well-to-do businessman in Sydney, arrived back, coming into the port of Crookhaven on a boat one day. At the port, he immediately saw its potential to make money selling produce to the ships stopping there, the last stop before going on to America.

"He'd brought a bag of gold back from Australia, and used that, along with his restless energy, to set about buying up lots of good land to grow produce to supply the ships.

"When Michael saw Neil sitting by the fire, doing nothing, the story is that he went out and cut Neil two walking sticks. He told him to stop feeling sorry for himself, to get up and get to work, that they had much to do together to make the farm pay. He said to the whole family they could make a good living if they only took the opportunity there before them.

"For three years, the two of them made their plans and did it all together, buying the best land to be had and selling the produce to the ships. After the three years,

Michael married a girl in Crookhaven. Her father ran the supply operation in the port. Michael moved there to run this, which prospered as did the farm.

"Both brothers still got on well, but I think it suited them each to have a different bit of the operation that was theirs, and by then, Michael was spending three quarters of his time in Crookhaven anyway.

"The woman Michael married was named Rose, and by all accounts, her beauty matched the name she carried, though it was said her character was more of a wild Irish rose than the soft English garden variety.

"Neil remained and ran the farm. With his walking sticks and his dray, he became as capable as any other man of the land. Over the next ten years, it's said he made a vast sum of money and used much of it to buy up all the best land nearby for his business.

"Along the way, he married a girl, also from a well-to-do family. She was as clever and hard working as he, and they had eight children, four boys and four girls, and built this fine house, which is all that remains of the lands today.

"In later years, times grew tough, first with the potato famine causing hunger and desperation, though the family tried to give food to the local poor. Then, after the coming of steamships, many ships stopped calling to Crookhaven to replenish supplies before their voyage on to America.

"Once Neil died, there were squabbles over the land and its management by his sons. In the end, most of it was sold off, its value divided between the surviving brothers, as was the way of the time.

"Neil's wife stayed on in the house with the youngest daughter, who was unmarried, after his death. The older sisters had all married by then and each moved away. The mother passed the house to her youngest daughter this way.

"Later, an unmarried niece became this daughter's companion and carer, and the house became hers in due course. Since that time, it has passed from relative to relative, following the female side of the family. It's remained a place for unmarried sisters and aunts to live, until this day.

"I'm the last of the line as far as I know. I had my own children early, and they've all moved far away, another generation of migrants. After my husband died, I came here to care for two elderly aunts and the house passed to me."

I can see there's barely enough money these days to pay for this grand house's upkeep. The gardens need tending, and many parts of the house need paint and repairs, but it looks as though Kathleen does her best, cleaning, polishing and keeping these antique fragments of history alive.

"If I was younger, I'd turn it into one of those grand Irish farm stay houses," she says. "Like the ones on TV. It's beyond me now, past eighty. Perhaps I'll find another in my scattered family to take it over and do this when I die. For now, I'm happy to tell its story to any who care to listen."

With the main story told, Kathleen pauses to drink her tea and give me a chance to think and ask questions.

"What happened to Michael after that? Do you know what became of him? Did he ever go back to Australia?"

"It seems he was always a restless soul, forever looking for a new opportunity. I don't rightly know, but it's said that after ten years in Crookhaven, he and his wife and their three children took one of the boats on to America to run the trading operation there, in a place like

New York or maybe Boston. By then the business had moved to supplying lots of produce out of Ireland for the American colonies.

"Those places had become the main destinations for waves of Irish migrants, many driven by the famine.

As they established their new lives there was an ongoing demand for things from the home country. Ever awake to a chance, Michael took it, or at least that's how the story goes. He and Neil are family heroes, remembered more through the retelling of old stories than through hard facts, though there's probably a kernel of truth in the stories."

"Did he ever return to Australia, do you know?"

"That I don't know, but there's a box of old papers, a diary, some letters and other bits and pieces at the house here. They were said to be things of his that got left here. Why he didn't take them with him when he married I don't know. I saw them a few years ago when I was cleaning the attic. I meant to read them but never got around to it. Would you like to have a look?"

I nod. "Yes please. That would be fascinating. Is there anyone else in the family I could ask about Michael who might know where he went? Any ancestors of his wife's family still in Crookhaven?"

She thinks for a minute then says, "I think her family were the Roches. Perhaps if you ask in Crookhaven there'll be someone like me who'll remember them, a person who knows where they went, settled, about the children and all."

Kathleen goes off to search for Michael's things. When she returns she hands me a box.

"Thank you. I promise to return it to you as soon as I've read its contents."

Chapter 34 – Josephine- Michael's Story

The box Kathleen handed to me is an old box of plain timber with a lock, though the key is long gone. Luckily, it's open, and inside is a leather-bound notebook and a bundle of papers about an inch thick.

As I open the notebook, I realise it's a diary detailing a decade of Michael's life. The final entry is dated Easter Sunday, 1832. It reads:

I have reached the grand old age of thirty some time last year, though I do not know the exact date of my birth. But my mammy used to say it was in early spring when the daffodils were out.

Now I have a family of my own, a wife, who custom dictates I cannot marry, and three brown children, who again custom dictates, I cannot claim as mine. I hate this stupid prejudice that I must marry and have children with a white lady, one who looks like me, in order to mix in higher society.

I do not have it in me to change the world, so I must go with it.

I wonder if I will ever see this family again. I left it in Sydney to return to the other one that I left behind in Ireland all those years ago.

It is wonderful to be returning to the land of my birth, but I miss the country and family I have left behind too. I must ensure they are safe and cared for while I am away. I have left them a bag of silver coins, maybe two to three hundred coins of fifty pounds in value. It should be enough to last them for one year, maybe two, while I am away. I had thought of giving them a bag of gold, but it's too dangerous. Paying in gold in Sydney, a town of thieves and scoundrels, would encourage every vagabond or robber to visit.

I have asked my friend, Robert, to look after them, at least to keep an eye on them and make sure nobody tries to take away my land or steal the produce they sell and, if needed, to advance them further money in lieu of my return. He will also manage the money coming from the sale of farm produce.

He will give them the main share, but keep a part for himself as his agent's fee. I trust him to do this with honesty and honour.

I put down Michael's diary, a bit overwhelmed with the emotions of reading this short entry. What about this family makes leaving loved ones their ongoing story, leaving by choice at times, but mostly by circumstance. Michael, a man transported in chains for being a wild teenager and stealing a pig, a man who returns to his Irish family out of duty, but in doing so, he leaves his new family behind. Subconsciously, I know Jim is his descendant, and that this pattern has flowed through to him: the leaving of his mother, torn from her family as a little child, followed by the leaving of the son, to support his wife and their tiny baby, only to return a month later and find they'd both permanently left him through circumstances beyond their control.

I too had my part to play in this by failing to hold on to my friend tightly enough when I could have. In this moment, I know enough leaving has been done. It can't go on any longer or happen again. It's my duty to break this cycle. It's for me to return to Jim.

I left him to salve my conscience, even though, deep down, I knew he needed me and I should stay. I see now that his history rendered him incapable of asking me to stay.

Before I return and ask Jim if he'll take me back, I'm going to follow the story of his family to where it ends, and in doing so, I'll hope to give him back his family's history and the full story of Michael O'Flaherty.

That night I read on until my eyes glaze, page after page of neat notation as Michael shares his memories of the boat trips of transportation, beginning with that from Ireland to the hulk in Portsmouth, and then the passage to Sydney.

His first entry is in 1819, the year after he arrived in Sydney. He says he's just bought a notebook in a market in Sydney. Despite his convict status, he has considerable freedom to come and go, as long as he comes to work when due, returns when due, and does his duty. He's housed in a convict barracks in Cockle Bay. Lord Macquarie is Governor and, with his wife, they have set about giving Sydney the many fine buildings it deserves, built of the local sandstone. To supply this sandstone, they've established quarries along this side of the harbour to mine its abundant stone and at the same time create better mooring points for ships, carved into the sandstone headlands.

The first night after Michael got his notebook he found a quiet corner of the barracks. In the candlelight, he wrote out his many memories of the trip and of his arrival in Sydney. He tells how, in the eight months since he reached there, he's made two good friends from Ireland, men who were both transported for similar crimes. They work alongside one another and keep a lookout for each other. They've been collectively named the Irish Brothers.

Michael writes about their assignment to the building of the Governor's Stables, the grandest building yet to be built in Sydney. He mockingly notes the horses there have a better life than most common people, better places to stay, better food, no floggings.

But it's clear that Michael and the other Irish Brothers are prospering. They've created their own mark of an Irish harp, cast into a chisel shaped tool of hardened steel that a blacksmith made them in return for a small cask of potcheen. Now they stamp it into stone blocks they shape and fit, as a record for posterity of their handiwork. Michael, musing, wonders whether, in two hundred years, somebody will remark on it and wonder who the stonemason was.

In a later entry, he talks about the grand day of the stable's opening, how they and the other workers stand at the back, listening to speeches from the Governor and other officials and how, soon after, at the urging of Francis Greenway, the architect and a former convict, the Governor grants them and a dozen other workers the remission of the remainder of their sentences as a reward for their good work on this fine building.

As freed men, they form a masonry building company, the Irish Brothers. Over the next two years they build another dozen fine houses, some for the government and others for wealthy settlers. By the end of this time, each has substantial savings, and a restless urge has come over the other two as they see good lands being granted to settlers in outlying regions. Each applies for and is granted his own parcel, Paddy to the north, and Billy over the mountains.

Michael sees plenty of opportunity in Sydney, so he continues the building company but soon also expands into the supply of fine liquor. It's blended from a mix of local ingredients, manufactured in his basement still, and fine imported liquor, which he secretly buys in casks from visiting ship's captains, free of tax. It's brought ashore at night, after tax inspectors have gone home or are in their cups, stored in a basement in the port until he collects it.

He buys out of the way land for a stonemason's yard and builds a still in the house basement, using the time-honoured methods of brewing superior potcheen, handed down from his grandparents in Ireland. He also experiments with and adds in local flavours that he sources from the aboriginal people who live nearby.

He has three premium brands, a fine Scotch whisky, a gin modelled on London Dry Gin but with local botanicals to give it a distinctive flavour, and an absinthe, sourced from an absinthe served in the finest Paris drawing rooms but again with his own local ingredients blended in.

His business supplies about twenty local drinking establishments, but only to those he knows and fully trusts, done through select middle men. All transactions are done on a gold coin basis, one large bottle of his best whisky for a sovereign, or two large bottles of gin or absinthe for the same price.

He also has market gardens on ten acres of his land from which he sells local produce into the markets in Sydney. He uses the surplus production for his stills. He also has a legal brewing business of inferior ale and spirits, which he sells openly with duty paid, as a legal cover for his superior product. It makes only a small profit, but, with his black labour force, the costs of production are minimal.

Increasingly, an aboriginal woman partner features in his writing. She's a niece of Bennelong, who he calls Yura, and an important person in the local community. Before long, she's running the aboriginal part of the enterprise and arranging workers each night in the basement, making sure they're paid and supervising the growing and selling of the garden produce. It seems she's a woman of status in the Sydney community and within the local tribe.

She becomes the mother of Michael's children. He writes of his pride as he watches her belly swell with their first child, and of how they now share a bed most nights.

He tells of his pleasure as he holds their newborn baby and then describes how he watches this child grow into a delightful son, full of endless mischief and chatter.

In time, they have a second child, a daughter, then another one. Michael laments the fact he cannot marry Yura in the same way he would if her skin was white, and also that he cannot recognise the children as his own on account of their mixed ancestry. It's a powerful, moving account of people trapped between two worlds, he an Irish convict made good, and she an original inhabitant of this land without any recognised status. How this would have played out in the end is uncertain, but for over five years this status quo seems to continue without incident.

Then come the final records of his letter from his parents, his decision to return to Ireland, and details of his final arrangements before he departed. He places all his savings, but for one bag of gold coins, in the basement, then works for two nights to lay a new floor over the old one. The only people who will know of the room beneath will be a handful of aboriginal workers and his wife. He trusts Yura not to tell, and the others do not have the English words to say anything even if they would.

He tells nobody, not even his Yura, of the gold. He covers the evidence to keep her and his children and the workers safe. If the English found the place, it would cause much trouble, so she must tell nobody.

Robbie, his former stone worker who now has his stonemason's business, will manage sales of the produce from the farm, making sure squatters don't impede farm operations or disturb the blacks. With that organised, Michael boards the ship and sails for England.

I know this part of the story, and it's largely complete. The only part missing is what happens to Michael after he goes to America and whether he ever returns to Australia. Perhaps more is to be gleaned from the pile of letters and other papers I've yet to read. As the night approaches dawn, my eyes begin to close. My next step will be to visit Crookhaven to see if I can take this story any further beyond what I've read here.

Chapter 35 – Josephine – American Connection

I sleep until lunchtime before I emerge, bleary-eyed, and drive the twenty miles drive to Crookhaven. Along the way, I marvel at the glorious coastal scenery. It's early spring. The sea sparkles in the bays and coastal idents, misty light flows softly down off rolling green hills with their rising piles of barren rocks.

I make a short detour to Barleycove and savour the fresh sea breeze whipping off the Atlantic breakers, which roll relentlessly in, sweeping along past the southern edge of the bay. A tourist sign says a tidal wave engulfed this coast centuries before. Despite the freezing cold water, three wild Irish children jump from a creek bank into the water as it flows along its narrow course into the ocean. Gulls and petrels screech as they circle in the air eddies above.

Crookhaven is a delight, a magical sheltered harbour tucked away from the raging ocean. I try to imagine it as an almost a solid wall of ships, as Michael described in his diary almost two centuries ago. Now all the bustle is gone. Crookhaven is back to a sleepy village nestled alongside the most perfect piece of protected water. It's afternoon tea time when I arrive. A scattering of tourists and locals take in the afternoon sea air, getting ready for a pint in a warm place out of the wind.

I choose the oldest looking hotel, which has an equally old man serving at the bar, and order myself an Irish Coffee, two buttered slices of brown soda bread and a bowl of fresh Irish seafood chowder. As I settle in, ready to enjoy my first food of the day, the barman rests his elbows on the counter and inquires what brings an Australian accent out here.

I decide the direct approach is best. "I'm here trying to locate a distant relative. He lived here nearly two hundred years ago. The story I was told is he married a Roche girl from around here. Her father ran a business provisioning the boats to America, way back then."

The barman scratches his head, then rubs his chin stubble, before saying, "Well, we've three Roches living in the town. Two are young and unlikely to be of much help, but there is old Mr Roche, bout my age he is. He used to be harbour master. These days he lives in the cottage closest to the harbour end of the town, a place where he can watch the ship comings and goings, a thing he's done all his life.

He normally wanders in for a pint of Guinness nigh on dusk, before he heads home to a pot of his wife's Irish Stew or something like. You could wait here, and I reckon you'll catch him in a couple hours' time, or you could head out there. He's probably having his afternoon tea as we speak. He's always good for a yarn.

I take him at his word and head off for the cottage. It turns out Mr Roche is descended from the wife, Rose's, brother. It's many generations back, but he still knows the story. Over the kitchen table, and a tarry pot of tea, he pulls out an old pouch of letters, passed down over four plus generations, written from his many times great aunt to her brother in his distant lineage.

I read a couple of letters, but there's only family chitchat with Michael mentioned in passing as Rose's husband. I quickly skim through the pile. The last letter is dated 1862. Rose tells her brother she's gravely ill, with her life coming to an end and Michael by her side.

The letter was sent from a small town called Deep River in Connecticut. Dr Google, on my phone, tells me this is village of great charm, with about five thousand people, which still retains much of its early historic character. It was once the American centre of the ivory trade, and so became very rich along the way.

It sounds like a tourist promo, but it's still worth a visit. I can fit that in before I fly back to Australia.

I find it amazing how often such distant places have preserved fragments of the past, often from times before where human memory can take us to.

That night, I return to visit Kathleen in her magic old house, sharing a pot of her stew and returning the diary and pages of letters, which I've carefully copied. She wishes me well and asks me to return and bring Jim, who I've told her briefly about, along with the fact he may be a distant descendant. "If he's an Australian descendant, perhaps he can inherit this house. As a young one, he'll have the energy to restore it to its former glory.

I laugh. "Who knows. If I have a say, Jim will surely visit, though he has enough with his own home restoration project to keep him busy at the moment."

Tomorrow, I'll drive to Limerick, where I'll stay for a night, after following around the Ring of Kerry. My flight departs the next day from Shannon Airport to New York, and I'll go on from there.

Three days later, I'm standing in the Deep River village square. It's as cute as the promotions attest. I have an address to visit, but I'll leave that to tomorrow.

Today I'll savour this slice of the past. It's time to stop and smell the roses and enjoy the best of what life offer, before I make my final effort to close this story.

I don't know why, but I've gained an unquenchable optimism that this is the end of the road, that an answer will lie here. It's based on nothing more than intuition, yet I really feel it will be so.

I play tourist for a few hours and then, in the late afternoon, I visit the village graveyard, neatly ordered, in many rows which belie the small population residing here. Long rows of headstones reveal its use over three hundred years, so its size is not really surprising.

Amongst the graves, I discover a succession of graves bearing the family name of O'Flaherty, running back to the 1860s. The earliest, in 1863, is that of Rose O'Flaherty, whose loss is grieved by her husband Michael and children Thomas, James and Sinead. A bit further along, I find these three children's graves, all in the 1890s, then other generations continuing on. There's no grave for Michael O'Flaherty, and no further reference to him except as the father of two of his children, Sinead and Thomas, but not of James, whose grave lies beside that of his mother. The other two children are buried around the corner from her in two adjacent plots, so it's clear that the family settled here and stayed over decades, even centuries, and that Michael lived here with Rose until 1863 when, by my calculations, he was sixty-two years old.

But it appears he did not die in America, so where did he go? Perhaps, if I can find some of his continuing family here, they'll know the rest of the story.

Next morning, I visit the address I've written down from the letter in Crookhaven. It's a grand house, though not so grand as the house in Ireland. It's clear it's changed over the last century with a modern wing out the back and a large garage off to the side, though many original features remain. Much of the building work looks modern, as if new owners in the last decade have set about transforming an old house.

I ring at the door. The lady who answers is in her fifties, clearly well-to-do, and yes, they bought the house about ten years ago when it was very run down.

"Did you know the previous owners? I'm trying to trace a branch of my family's history."

"No, not at the time when we bought it. It was a deceased estate, not lived in for several years. Perhaps the real estate agent who sold it to us might know."

There's nothing friendly in her manner which, after the warmth of the Irish, makes me feel sad. I feel little optimism the real estate agent will be any more help, so I turn to the local phone book. It has more than a dozen O'Flaherty's. I ring my way down the list.

Some people I speak with are suspicious and some are genuinely helpful. Most know nothing of great grandparents or beyond, though a couple think they may have come out from Ireland a long time ago and that they once owned the grand house I visited, though it's not been in their family for a long time.

I have two names left, a Margaret O'Flaherty and another listed as J O'Flaherty. I dial the last and wait.

An older man answers, with the old patrician accent one still finds in out of the way places. "Hello, James here, and how can I help you?"

I explain my purpose, as helping a friend try and trace a distant relative from the 1800s. It seems he's at least of the right family, with some knowledge going back. "Well, actually, my great grandfather was James O'Flaherty. It's said he was the son of Michael, and we've passed the name James down through each generation since, though I've only daughters, so it ends with me. I suppose you could say I'm James O'Flaherty Four," he says with a slight chuckle.

After a few minutes of conversation about the family's fortunes, which are considerable, and of the scattering of relatives across the area, we get to the point of the missing grave of Michael.

"There's a family story about what happened, though I'm not sure how much's true. But you're right, he left town after Rose died. His son James was always angry about it. As middle boy, he was his mother's favoured son. He thought it shameful that, with his mother barely buried, his father abandoned his family and went off across the world, never to return. Of course, the family was all well grown by then; each child was married with their own children and doing well. It was hardly abandonment.

"I've heard that he headed on to California and from there took a boat to the Antipodes, perhaps Australia or New Zealand, and was never heard of again. That's not really true. He did send an occasional letter to his daughter, Sinead, which he asked her to pass on to her brothers to tell them what he was doing. As far as I know, James never read the letters and all the letters vanished. He stayed angry with his father for the rest of his life 'for running away from family duties', was how he put it.

"Great Aunt Sinead never told the others of their content, though Thomas is said to have read them too. Apparently, there was a dark secret in them that she didn't want the wider family to know. It seems that knowledge died with her, that's unless her brother Thomas told someone, but if he did, I've never heard of it. Perhaps the letters were burned after reading."

"Is there anyone else in the family who is likely to know anything more?"

"Sadly, I don't think so. The only reason the story has passed down is because great grandfather James stayed angry all his life with his father, and when he died, he gave specific instructions that he didn't want his father's name on his headstone. So, it's become a quirky family story that lives on, even though the rest of the memory has gone."

So here I am at the end of the trail. I have part of an answer, but not quite enough to finish the story. Michael left America after his wife died. He travelled on, perhaps back to Australia. But to where and why?

It's like peeling an onion; as each layer is removed a bit more is revealed, but still, at the centre, some part remains hidden. Perhaps I'll just have to accept that the mystery at the core will forever be beyond knowing.

In any event, it's nearly time to return to Australia, to my home and the man I love, and to share with him what I've discovered. That prospect excites me.

But at the same time I'm disappointed. I've tried so hard to help uncover his story, to give Jim back his history. A day ago, I was sure of success. Today, I see it's merely castles in the air, hopes created within my mind based on nothing real.

Without an ending, what I've uncovered feels empty. I must get used to the idea that I'm not Jim's saviour. It's good I don't return with any sense of inflated importance.

Jim and I were so close before. I hope we can be lovers and friends again, maybe more, but I'm not quite ready to fully open my heart again to him again.

Disappointment hurts me too much as well. So, for now, I'll continue my travels in North America. I've always wanted to see the snowy north, perhaps Canada and Alaska. I've heard of people who take a cruise up the inside passage from Seattle or Vancouver, going to places where the orcas frolic and mighty forests fringe high snowy mountains. There say there are sparkling harbours, bears, whales and drifting icebergs to see. My mind tells me to take this trip.

When it's done, I think I'll be ready to go home.

Chapter 36 – Jim – The Finding of Nothing

A third month has gone by since the excavation started. We have found little that's new. At the start, we found a letter to Michael from a priest in Ireland asking him to come home because his family needed him. The envelope this letter potentially arrived in was addressed to Michael O'Flaherty, and the priest who sent it was in the town of Schull or Skull in the south of Ireland.

Since then, we've been through lots of other papers, but they have little more to tell. They're not personal, just things like payment receipts, orders, invoices, papers about the running of a farm and what appears to be an illicit still selling its products across Sydney town and its surrounds throughout the mid to late 1820s. There are also some drawn to scale plans for houses and other building documents, but they're older as if this work predates the other business.

I have puzzled a bit over why Michael didn't label the spirits with his name, choosing instead 'Michael Kelly's Superior Whiskey, Gin and Absinthe. He was clearly a canny man. Perhaps having his own name on the label may have been too high risk, especially if it got into the wrong hands. Kelly is the ubiquitous Irish name, given to outlaws and innumerable others, so this label tells a story of Irish heritage without implicating him directly. And many bottles have no labels at all, perhaps they were sold to others to use their own labels, and keep his role in their provenance unknown.

The whole thing is like a jigsaw puzzle with most pieces missing. We see half shapes of people who lived here and worked over a decade, but nothing to tell us how they came to be here or where they went. And why did they seal up this veritable treasure trove and never return for the booty?

Meanwhile, Kate has set two of her students to work on related projects, one to research the early ownership transactions for the house, and one to search for other clues, things like the reason the railway was built around the house, what other houses nearby are shown in early town plans, who built them and what happened to the farm and its produce.

I'm betting the original house owner was Michael O'Flaherty, and he was a builder, stone mason, illegal still owner and a probable member of the Irish Brothers gang around the 1820s. There's a suggestion from the letter that he returned to Ireland in about 1830 to help with a family crisis, but what happened afterwards?

He was clearly a very wealthy man by then, in both the measures of that day and as counted today. Eight bags of gold was a real pile, not to mention the value of the house, bottled spirits and whatever else he owned.

But it's like someone flipped the light switch on for a decade, and then turned it off again, giving a snapshot of that distant time but nothing before or after to give it a broader reference or meaning.

The excavation's done, so I've been given back the use of my house. Various historic objects found in the cellar, to which I don't want to lay claim, have been removed and taken to a storage vault at the Australian Museum. Each one was carefully labelled, photographed in situ, and its information recorded and catalogued before leaving here.

I've put a table and two chairs down in the cellar now, and I use it as my private space for when I want to sit and think or maybe write down a few things. My ideas flow freely when sitting there amongst all these ghosts of a distant past.

Kate and Marti have become as thick as thieves. They make lots of plans that go around me. I don't really mind; at such times ignorance is bliss.

They are working together on the publicity for our find. It's not got out yet, but it's only a matter of time. Too many people know far too much by now to keep it buried. If they don't put the real story out soon, an unofficial one, full of wild speculation will take its place. I don't care which way it happens and no longer care much about how the story runs. Nobody's any the wiser about our gold hoard, and it can stay that way for now.

If the media want to interview me about the discovery, that's fine. I'll spin them a yarn about long lost Irish relatives. I'd like to know who they were, how they came here and where they went, but that's what other people are working on. Anyway, this secret has been buried for almost two hundred years, so another week, month or year matters little.

Two things occupy my mind at present. The first is the other house that's been found, the childhood home where my mother briefly lived. I'd like to have it back in our family, though its price will be a big number that I doubt I can raise, even factoring in the buried million and other buried treasures. But, still, I want it as a memento of my mother, the place of her happy childhood memories.

Perhaps Kate could own it and keep the family connection going. I'd love it to be my first true gift to her, the same way as in olden times dowries were given, not that she's getting married or needs a dowry, as the self-made independent woman she is. Perhaps I'll talk to Marti and Ellie, or even to Kate's parents and my

Brisbane relatives, to see if, somehow, we can put together enough funds to buy it back for the family.

The second thing on my mind is how to get Josephine back. When she first went away, I was too shocked to think through what to do.

I know Kate was trying to play matchmaker, but it's not for her to bring me and Josephine back together. I love Kate and she are friends, as if daughter and mother. But what's grown between me and Josephine is for ourselves alone.

I've run away from fighting for those I love for far too long and looking back at those brief few days when we were together, I know that, for the first time since Cindy, love is truly what it was.

Josephine was always beautiful, and I remember the attraction there was between us back then before I met Cindy. Her beauty today is as undiminished. That night, when she took my hand and brought me to her bed for comfort, as we both searched for the elusive Cindy, it was like a fire caught inside me. It was the same every new day after that. She had only to look at me and my day came alive. The smell of her hair, the touch of her hand, the feel of her warm body joined to mine; all were equally wonderful.

But I was temporarily paralysed by the shock of her leaving and so I let her leave without trying to find a way to save what we had.

Now it's up to me to act, to go and find her, to bring back her home with me and cherish her forever.

I only hope she still wants me.

Chapter 37 – Marti – To Buy a House

It seems that great minds think alike, and all our minds have coalesced on one thing: to buy the house next door and return it to our family. All of us really want the house to belong to Kate. Ellie and I have talked it through. We're both determined to try. Jim is now in on the plan too.

The gold is the backstop. We know it's there and have a fair idea of its raw value, the price paid for the metal content, not a collector's price, which would likely be much more. If needed, we could also auction the two hundred and fifty bottles of aged whisky, gin and liqueur, which would be likely to fetch a tidy sum. Estimates are upwards of one thousand dollars a bottle, maybe substantially more.

Our short term estimate is we need one and a half to two million dollars to be successful bidders at the auction next week. Because we have assets rather than liquid cash, we need a bank to back us. My mother owns her house next door outright, so she's using it to provide a guarantee for a loan of a million that I've been able to secure from the bank. She's also come up with $100,000 from her private savings, as have I and Sharon from Brisbane, so we have $300,000 to cover the required deposit. Jim has raised a loan of $200,000, based on his income and unrealised assets of two hundred and fifty bottles of spirits. It feels a bit like the good old days when you passed the hat around to whip up some cash for a shout of drinks. Although this round is a little more expensive. But all up, we've come up with one and a half million dollars.

The house is described as a turn of the 20th century magnificent Victorian terrace, built over three levels on a large block and located in a leafy quiet street in Redfern. Its enchanting garden is featured heavily in the real estate agent's advertisement. Providing the house doesn't rise above $1.5 million, we have the means to buy it back. I just hope there aren't too many other cashed up bidders. I'll cross all my fingers and toes.

I've asked a real estate friend to bid on our behalf. I don't want the owners to know we're bidders, lest they feel under pressure to give us the house on the cheap. I know they need the sale money for their retirement.

On the day of the auction, the house owners fly back from Perth. They tell us that three local parties, who appear to have both the interest and the means, have inspected the house and are registered as bidders. There are another two registered bidders who they don't know anything about, other than that one is bidding from overseas through a buyer's agent. I am guessing that one of the unknown bidders is my real estate friend. The other is a mystery.

The owners, still our close friends, tell us they'd be happy with $1.4 million, though they've set the reserve a little higher to give room for private negotiation. Ellie and I, who stand side by side chatting to them as a crowd gathers, stay silent. Jim and Kate, each standing separate, are right up the back of the crowd, as are Kate's parents.

None of us have given Kate a clue to our intentions.

Five minutes after the due time, the auctioneer calls the crowd to order. We're all in the back garden, arranged around the middle courtyard under its canopy, the agent on the level below us. It's a lovely autumn day with the leaves above and around us tinged with red and gold, as they filter muted light.

The agent starts his rev-up speech. He highlights the beautiful period features of the house and goes into paroxysms of exuberance at its garden, "An Italian Palace garden masterpiece, modelled after all the great houses and palaces of Italy, in which the builders, two Italian brothers, first worked, before coming to Australia."

Then it is time for the bidding to begin. The opening gambit is for one million dollars, and before long, the bidding is underway. One point one, one point two, one two fifty, one two seventy. I pray the bidding is slowing down.

Once bidding drifts past the one point three mark, our bidder interjects and bumps it up to one point four. Almost before I can blink, the price has run up to one point five, and we're not holding the bid. My agent looks at me inquiringly. I nod and show five fingers. She comes in again at one five fifty. It is fifty more than I really have. I'm sure I can fudge it somehow, but it's my absolute limit. For a few seconds, there's silence, and I dare to hope.

Then it's off again and is soon past one point six and then up to one point seven. There are only two bidders left in the running, and both are going up in ten thousand-dollar increments. Bidding stalls when it hits one point eight. I wonder whose nerve will hold.

The agent for the under bidder is on the phone. There is a half murmur from the crowd when he puts up two fingers. I think it means one eight two, and that's what the agent calls out, but the bidder shakes his head. "No, two million dollars is the offer."

There's a half gasp from the crowd and then it's all over as the agent calls out, "Going once, going twice, all done, sold! Sold to Registered Bidder Six, ringing in from America, an Australian who says she wants to return home. I'm sure she will love this property."

The owners are beside themselves with delight as they chat to me and Ellie. We make a good fist of sharing their delight, despite the sour taste of disappointment at the back of our throats.

After a few minutes, the agent comes over and says the owners, "The purchaser has lodged the ten percent deposit bank cheque with us. She's asked if we would consider having settlement in thirty days not the customary forty-two days, that's if you'll agree.

"She's due to fly back to Australia in three weeks, so she's hoping for settlement a week after her return. She'd like to take vacant possession as soon after that as can be arranged."

It is all agreed.

As the owners want to fly back to Perth tomorrow, they ask Ellie if, when the new owner arrives, we could welcome her on their behalf as our new neighbour and introduce her to others around the locality.

We agree we'll make the buyer feel welcome.

Chapter 38 – Josephine – Alaska

Over the last month, I've enjoyed a two-week trip across North America, first a train journey from New York through the upstate along the Hudson River, followed by a visit to Chicago, and around the Great Lakes with a stopover at Niagara Falls, before catching the Empire Builder Train across the continent, passing wonders such as Glacier National Park and the Rocky Mountains, en route to Seattle.

There I boarded a two-week cruise to Alaska. It's almost at an end now as we sail up the Cook Inlet approaching Anchorage, passing seals and occasional whale breaches as we work our way along these sheltered waters. Our backdrop is the towering snow-covered mountains which ring the town, forming a picture postcard image.

There's much to be said for the pleasure of having enough money not to worry about the cost. It's my great freedom. My first husband didn't have many redeeming features, God rest his scummy soul. But the generosity of his divorce settlement was one big plus when he traded me in for a younger model. I was forty and had been with him for nearly fifteen years, while she was barely out of her teens. Their relationship lasted a decade before a sudden heart attack found him pushing up daisies. But it left me with a house in one of the best parts of Mosman, which is conservatively worth four to five million. I also inherited a cash settlement of over another million.

Last month, deciding I didn't need a house so grand, I put it on the market. Within a fortnight, it sold for the upper end of its valuation, a whisker shy of the five million. The settlement is next week, after which the money will be deposited into my bank account. I feel free to spend a good portion of my inheritance on travel or any other things that take my fancy.

My brother inherited the family farm out past Wagga when my Dad, after years working as an alcoholic shearer, died a few years ago, twenty years after Mum, who had stayed on the farm. There are five of us children and three grandchildren, who I love to see on my visits. They're a good substitute for children of my own, and now Kate feels like a daughter too.

Perhaps I'll buy a hundred acres of land west of the mountains, enough space to run a few horses, sheep and cattle, without the hard work required to run a proper farm like what my brother has. It will be a place with a comfortable old farmhouse and a shed with tools for a handy man around the house. I dream I've found this man. I can do this for inside a million, so that leaves money to make other investments in the city as well as plenty of spare cash to live well on. And I still have my interior design business in Mosman, with a part time manager, which earns me a good income. These are reasons why I can afford to take holidays and travel without counting the cost, and why, when I get home, I'm looking forward to buying a new home.

This trip is almost at an end as we approach Anchorage Harbour, where I'm disembarking. I have three nights in Anchorage before I begin the return leg to Oz. I need to be back in Sydney before next weekend when I have an engagement I can't miss.

This last month has all been wonderful, the scenery, the company, the food. Both Americans and Canadians are very gracious hosts. They could teach our English and European cousins a thing or two about manners and politeness.

Yet, despite this, I have a hole in my heart where Jim's smiling face belongs. I know I had to find my own place of inside quiet, to let ghosts of the past find peace, but I have an unquiet fear that running away from him was foolish.

Kate assures me, in her regular emails, that there's nobody new. Yet she also told me, in a disturbing email last week, that he's gone off travelling by himself. He wouldn't tell her where to. All I know is that he's due back in Sydney around the time I am and that he needed an Australian passport in a big rush before his trip.

Perhaps, following up on my information on Michael, which Kate told me she passed on, he's gone to the same places I visited in Ireland, to see if he can find out any more for himself.

I can only hope he doesn't meet somebody new on his travels and lose interest in me. Maybe I would deserve it though, after leaving him without a word.

I'm lost in thoughts of what ifs as I pack my luggage and get ready for departure from the boat. When I've got it all bagged and ready, I follow the others down the gangplank into the shore-side concourse, where a mass of people are swirling around waiting to greet the new arrivals.

Suddenly, standing directly in front of me, is a man.

It's the body of a large familiar man, and his arms are open to welcome me. Jim came here to find me.

My heart explodes with joy. He sweeps me up and swings me round, like a child, with effortless strength.

We talk little as he brings me back to his hotel room, a penthouse suite with views across the bay to the mountains beyond, and brings me to his bed. We barely see the view outside as time stands still and we lose ourselves in each other. Now I know I'm really home.

Jim tells me of the plans he's made, using up most of his remaining savings to do a trip to the mountains, to see the bears catch salmon in their spawning run, ride a sled pulled by a husky team, pay for a helicopter to drop us into wilderness where we'll ski down a mountain. It's perfect, this way to start to our life together, the honeymoon I've always wanted.

The next day, before we head away, we each buy a ring for the other to wear. They're a promise that we'll formalise our relationship one day soon.

Chapter 39 – Kate – My Home

A gorgeous gold embossed envelope arrived at each of our houses yesterday. Inside was a gilt-framed card with a photograph of the house next door to Ellie and Marti's on it, and a message which read:

The new owner of this house politely requests the pleasure of your company at the property at 2 pm for afternoon refreshments.

There is no name and no further details provided.

It's seriously strange.

Though they're putting a brave face on it, I can tell that Jim, Ellie, Marti, and my parents are bitterly disappointed not to have bought the house themselves. It was only after the auction was over I discovered they'd all pooled their money to try buy it. I only wish they'd let me in on the secret so I could have added in more funds of my own.

Still, they're too polite to be ungracious to the new owner, and they're hoping that, when we meet this person, she will become a friend and care for the house in the way it deserves. I do love the house and wish it could have been returned to our family, but I have no sense of entitlement to it. It's simply a beautiful object that should be treasured by whoever owns it.

Before the 2.00 pm gathering, I go to Ellie's house to have brunch with Ellie, Marti and Jim. My mum and dad will meet us just before two, as they're also on the invitation list. The only one missing from our circle for the house visit is Josephine, who has some prior business or other.

Perhaps she's organising tonight. She's invited us all to some fancy restaurant for dinner on her and Jim's behalf. The invitation sounds like a big deal, price no object. I think it's like an engagement party, though not quite so formal yet.

Since I met Jim and Josephine off the plane two days ago, giving them both a huge hug, I've barely seen them. They've been inseparable in their new-found love, which totally delights me. It's a beautiful thing to see. A new part of our family. Jim has promised me a day with just him tomorrow, that this will be our time for a private catch up with each other to share all our news.

When brunch is finished and my parents have arrived, we each freshen up quickly and head next door.

Whoever has bought it has made a huge effort. It's neat as a pin. The walls are scrubbed and the trim repainted, the gardeners have been in, and every shrub is trimmed, every path swept and every bed weeded.

The front is festooned with balloons and streamers and an array of sparkling fairy lights. It looks like Christmas decorations times ten. The door has a big banner saying, 'Welcome Home', which feels weird.

We ring the bell. In a minute a butler, dressed in white livery, opens the door. He ushers us to a living room which is made up like a period piece from a fashion magazine with superb furnishings and other decorative touches.

The butler directs each of us to a deginated seat.

The seat I'm led to looks like the guest of honour's seat, a formal lounge chair facing the other seats. I sit down feeling this is becoming stranger and stranger.

We sit in a circle, all silent, as we watch and wait for whatever is set to unfold. It feels like the opening scene of a theatrical performance.

A lady, dressed to the nines in sequins and pearls, with her hair buried in a piled-up wig, enters carrying a silver tray which bears a single sheet of paper.

She walks to where I am sitting and indicates that I should remove this piece of paper from the tray.

It's then I recognise that the paper is the title deed of this house. And the name on the title deed is mine.

I look up. The person bearing the tray is Josephine.

"Welcome to your new home, Kate. It seemed fitting it should return to you, great grand-daughter of the family who first built it and who once lived here."

I can only shake my head in stunned silence before I finally stand and hug my new second mother.

This really is some present.

Chapter 40 – Jim - A Buried Story

Josephine and I have been married for a month now. After the ceremony, we set off on a two-week honeymoon to Ireland to meet all of our extended relatives living there.

From my brief time there, I love these Irish folks. Their sense of fun beats all, despite their country's tragic history. The loss of a quarter of their population to famine and another quarter to immigration in the years that followed, along with their never-ending fights with their British former landlords, running on through over four hundred years of history have not diminished their love of life.

I think that much of Australian national character, the mateship and contempt for superiority, were forged by the Irish in our country. When, at four in the morning, they sing the song, "Go on home, British soldiers, go on home, have you got no bloody homes of your own," my voice sings along with the best of them.

And I love the sequel when the publican wants to call it a night and shouts out, "Have ye got no homes to go to?" The response of course is a new bout of singing breaking out. I realise their rebellion runs deeper than against the English. It's rebellion in their souls to anyone spoiling the fun, and I'm good with that.

I don't know how I relate to these Irish folks, but it's clear my house has been in the family all along, from what we have found out so far, though there are gaps and bits that don't make sense.

The title, which was first issued in Michael O'Flaherty's name passed, without any money paid, but with a registered transfer, to a Stephen Keegan listed as a grandson, in 1902, presumably at some time after the death of Michael, though there's no record of this, or of Michael's return or further residence in Australia.

While we were away, Kate moved in with Marti and Ellie. It was amicable with her parents, though I'm more than sure they'll miss her. Kate and Marti have decided to turn Kate's house into an Airbnb, except for the top room with the wonderful bird painting. Kate will use this as her bedroom for the odd occasions she stays there when the house is unoccupied. The rest of time this room will be kept closed and locked to protect it.

Kate says she could not bear to have anyone to mark or other wise damage the beautiful bird painting on the amoire, which she calls Rachel's Treasure.

Kate and Marti will jointly manage the rest of property for short-term stays, making sure to vet applicants so as to ensure guests care for the property when they stay.

As for Josephine and I, we've moved back into my old house and are working together to make minor modifications, the main one being to build a new kitchen, dining room, and bathroom out the back, nothing too grand, but with sufficient comfort and space for us to entertain.

The basement will be our office and informal relaxing room, as well as a wine cellar using existing bottle shelves along one wall. The old living room will be our formal drawing room, which Josephine has decorated it with period furniture. It looks great.

We've worked together on the minor renovations to the main house but have builders doing the part out the back. We've also made plans to build a flower garden in the back yard, enclosed in a brick wall that hides away the railway surrounds. I have two tradie mates who'll do the brickwork, and the garden will be a joint project for Josephine and I to work on together. She, after all, is a farmer's daughter and loves to get her hands dirty in the soil. And her creative soul loves making beautiful spaces using flowers in the same way my mother once did.

As for the story of the house, it did make a brief front page splash in the papers, where it was described as the discovery of one of Sydney's earliest houses.

Kate and I did a few interviews with the press, but interest soon faded. Now it's just another old story, pushed aside by stories of new wars and politicians vying to lie. That suits me fine.

One day soon our extended family will decide what to do with the gold and the hundreds of bottles of spirits. We shared one on our wedding night, but otherwise they sit in storage, dusty and untouched.

On the day we start work on the new garden, we agree we need to remove all the rubbish, a mix of rocks and debris that cover the back yard, and put several truckloads of good soil in its place. It's feels like there's a hundred years of accumulation to shift, but I want to go slowly, taking it out, wheelbarrow by wheelbarrow load, to put into a skip, lest there be some historical pearls among the dross.

I don't know what I expect to find, perhaps some old stonemason's tools or aboriginal artefacts, based on the story that Michael's notebook tells.

I begin at the very back and dig out the foot of topsoil. After this layer is gone, we're down to an unbroken layer of old clay along with odd rock remnants which predate the house. We'll spread a three-foot-thick layer of good soil onto this newly cleared space, the sort that garden plants love.

The first day I remove this top layer from the back two metres of the yard, I find nothing of value. The second day, I work my way forward. The digging gets slower as the garden gets wider. By afternoon, I've removed another metre to half way across. As I swing my mattock to loosen the next bit of whatever's there, the steel blade gives a loud metallic clang. *Another bloody big lump of sandstone.*

I scrape around it to see where the end is, but this bit is different. It's a square slab, a bit like the stones under the basement floor. This one has ornate edges, as if a mason carved a fancy pattern into the stone.

I call Josephine over to have a look, and we work together to uncover it. At first, it's just a rectangular block of stone, about three feet wide. It extends back towards the house, with its fancy scrolled edge extending along both sides. Halfway along, we uncover an inscription carved into the stone. We keep clearing the topsoil away until the full length is revealed.

Now, Josephine gets a broom and brush and carefully removes all the remaining soil and rubbish from the surface.

The stone is a bit over two metres long and a metre wide. It slowly dawns on us that we're looking at the top of the vault of an old grave, a capstone which covers whatever lies buried below. On the grave are two inscriptions.

The first inscription, carved in beautiful cursive script reads:

Here lies Yura Warawee, beloved wife of Michael
Died 30th November 1875
Proud mother of Maria, Connor and Angela.
May God and her Spirit Ancestors
Keep her safe until we meet again

Below it sits a second inscription carved in a less expert hand, which reads:

Rest in Peace in God's Care
Michael O'Flaherty, aged 101 years.
Born 1801, died 20th September 1902.

Chapter 41 – Jim - Story of My Mother

Another month has gone by. We are seeking Heritage permission to open the grave and see what lies in it, which is no easy matter to gain.

Some people make suggestions that it should not be further disturbed out of respect for those who lie here.

I have little regard for the view that it should remain unopened, those who occupy it are not in a position to care after over a hundred years. And I'm sure there will be more clues inside it as to why it came to be here.

We will, of course, open the grave respectfully in acknowledgement of my distant antecedents.

In the meantime, Tommy Hass, from my home town, called. He's been diligently working for months to try trace anybody who knew my mother. He thinks he's struck gold, finding an old friend called Linda who knew my mum in her early days when she first moved out west. They were close friends for five years before Linda moved to another town.

In a lucky coincidence, Linda is coming to Sydney next Monday, and she's asked to meet me. I can't remember her, but I must have been no more than five when she left town, so that's no surprise.

I wonder how well she knew my mother, whether she knows how she came to live in the town of my birth and most particularly what made her so angry with both her relatives and the world of men.

Linda and I meet at the Newtown Hotel, a quiet place on weekdays. We find seats on its lovely wide upstairs veranda.

On seeing her I guess that Linda is probably in her late-seventies, a bit bird like with grey wiry hair and clear sharp blue eyes. She has the fierce gaze of a take no prisoners' person. I can see she'd have been very pretty in her youth, she's still striking today. I hope I'm as good at her age.

After brief introductions, Linda hands me a small battered suitcase she's brought with her. "I've been wanting to give you this for years, but I never knew where you'd gone until Tommy finally found me.

"It wasn't until a month after your mother died that I heard of her passing. The next weekend, I drove to the town to see if I could do anything to help. They were cleaning out the cottage that day. The only thing of hers with any value was this suitcase, not money value but memory value. It holds her scrap book, some letters and a few other things she kept. That day, I took it with me out of fear that someone would throw it out.

I had a mind to give it to you. But when I asked, nobody could say where you'd gone. All they knew was that you'd caught the train to Sydney. No one had seen nor heard hair nor hide from you since you'd left.

So the suitcase stayed with me all these years. I never threw it out, I reckoned that one day I'd run you to ground. Didn't realise it'd take nearly forty years to do, but here it is."

I set the case on the table and open it carefully. There, as remembered, is my mother's scrapbook, with the beautiful bird picture glued inside the front cover.

She nods as I lift it up and open it. "She'd have wanted you have that."

I flick through the contents. It's a mix of old photos, her drawings and other things that stare back at me. I feel a lump in my throat. These things are unbelievably precious to me, a collection of what captivated my mother when she was younger than Kate is now.

I turn to Linda. We both have tears in our eyes.

I say, "I don't know how to thank you. I forgot about this when I left, but I'm so glad you've minded it and brought it back to me. I have no words good enough to say how much it means to me."

She rests her hand on my arm. "God rest her, she was a good, kind soul, taken too soon. One who smiled each day, despite her rotten fate. Even when there was nothing to smile about, she'd stop and smell the flowers in her garden, smile and say, "Isn't that so beautiful!

"I hoped she and Tommy would get together in the end. If life was kinder to her, perhaps they would have. Tommy thought the sun shone from her eyes. But it was not to be."

We fall to talking, and I ask her, "Can you tell me about my mother's life before I was born?"

She nods. "Sure, it's in there, in the letters and documents, at least parts. Why don't you read it first and then we can talk again? Maybe I can fill in a few gaps. I'm staying on in Sydney for another week to catch up with a few nieces and nephews, so ring me when you're ready, and we'll meet again.

That night I sit in the cellar where the ghosts of so many people past enfold me with their presence.

Josephine sits in the chair alongside me, flicking through the scrapbook, laughing at odd things captured in it, smiling at others.

I work my way through the letters and documents.

They only give fragments, but these are enough.

Each fragment is its own story, something that mattered in another time and place and begin to explain.

There's my original birth certificate, signed by a sister in Moree hospital, with her name, Rachel Martin and the statement 'Father Unknown'.

There are a couple notes and letters between her and Linda, plans to meet together and share their news. I flick through these and put them aside.

I discover a letter from her, signed Rachel, written a few months before I was born to a James Irwin.

It is short and to the point.

Well, James,

It may come as a surprise to you to know that our nights spent together have had a result inside my belly. A baby is growing there.
As there's been nobody else, I guess that makes you the father.
When we were doing it, you told me how much you loved me.
I did love you too, to let you have your way.
But, seeing as how you're paying me little notice of late, I doubt that what you said to me then is true.
I know your family wants you and that girl on the station next door to get married, rather than you and the governess.
So the choice is yours. I won't ask for help again. It's my problem.
I'll have the baby on my own if you don't want to know about it.

Your once friend and lover
Rachel

Then there is the little scrap of paper in a childish hand,

I hate my sister so much.
She promised not to let them take her away from me, she said that we would stay together and she would look after me.
SHE LIED
And she knew our stepdaddy never hurt our mother.
Mummy was drunk and fell down the stairs. He never hit her.
SHE LIED ABOUT THAT TOO
So they took him away and put him in jail.
Then they took us away too – it's all her fault.
I hate her double.

Two days later, I meet Linda again. As we sit and talk, she dredges her memory for various things my mother told her. She tells how they were governesses on adjoining stations. They met doing School of the Air training in Moree and stayed friends afterwards, catching up whenever they could meet in a town or at a country social like a B & S Ball.

That was when my mother was fifteen and Linda seventeen. They stayed good friends for the rest of my mother's life, although when I was five Linda got married to the son of the station owner where she was working. Soon after they moved to another family property three hours' drive south. After that, they mostly talked on the telephone or sent letters.

As a farmer's wife, for the next few years, Linda was very busy raising her own children, so her chances to catch up with my mother after that were limited. But in the early years, they would use part of their precious wages to rent a hotel room together when they were both in town for a night, so they could keep in touch.

"It was a great comfort to me to have your mother as a good friend. I hope it was the same for her too."

I question what she knows of my mother's early life.

She tells me how awful the foster parents who raised her were, treating her like a domestic servant, giving her all the awful jobs, while their own children did nothing. It went on year after year and never improved.

"She did get two letters from her older sister Jane, delivered through the foster agency. They weren't allowed to write to each other directly. It seems Jane was the lucky one. Her own foster parents were kind and her life was good. She was having music lessons and learning to dance. The family had legally adopted her.

"I think your mother felt betrayed by Jane because after they got taken into care, when Jane was six and your mother was four, Jane had promised her that she'd not let them be separated and yet they had been.

And now all Jane did was brag about how good her own life was, when your mother's was awful. It made her so angry that she couldn't bear to read any letters ever again. After the first two, when other letters came, she'd never opened them but burned them in the fire.

"As your mother matured, the foster parents' son, who was two years older, would touch her breasts and between her legs when nobody else was around.

"It finally got too much for her one night, when the foster parents were away, he broke through the lock on her door, pulled her nightclothes off and tried to force himself on her. She fought back, scratching his face with her nails, and somehow she managed to wriggle out from underneath him. She ran out of the front door with only a towel around her and never went back there.

"She lived on the streets for a few weeks, stealing food and raiding rubbish bins to survive. Then she saw an advertisement in a discarded newspaper for a governess job out near Moree. She rang the number and they offered her the job on the phone and paid for a railway ticket for her to travel out, arranging for her to collect it at Central Station.

"She stayed there for a couple years. It was okay until the family's older son left school and came home to work on the farm. Soon it started again, the same way as it had with the foster brother, him always trying to get her alone to do unwanted things to her.

"She found another job. This time the job was good and the people seemed good. She was teaching the younger children their lessons and helping with the domestic work. She was eighteen when she started to notice the older brother, who was twenty-one.

"He was engaged to the girl on the property next door. He seemed kind and decent, and they spent more and more time together. One day he told her he didn't want to marry the girl next door because he liked her much better, and he wanted to go out with her instead.

"The other girl was away at university, studying an agriculture course, so often, during the days, it was only the two of them around.

She started doing more and more things with him, and all the while, he told her, over and over, how beautiful she was and how he would break off with the other girl when she came home on holiday.

"Because of all the promises he made, she finally relented and let him come into her bed for a few nights when his parents were away. For those few nights, it was wonderful and they told each other of their love. But once his parents came back it seemed he lost his interest in her.

Now all that was talked about was the plans for the wedding that Christmas, how wonderful it would be when the two properties were joined together. James seemed embarrassed by her now and would actively avoid being alone with her.

"When she knew she was pregnant, in desperation, she wrote him a letter. His mother returned it, unread by James, the next day. She told your mother she was a slut and said it was time to pack her bags and leave.

She drove her to town and left her in the main street with one hundred dollars.

"A couple times James came to town and tried to talk to her, asking what was wrong. But she refused to even look at him. When he saw she was pregnant, he asked if the baby was his. She denied it, saying she'd shagged a shearer newly come to town, that he was a much better fuck and James should leave her alone and marry the girl his family wanted.

"So that was that, she never spoke to him again, and she put around the shearer story. Despite it all, she named you James. She told me you were entitled to that one thing from your father, his name, but that was all.

"It's funny she called me Jim, not James," I say.

"Oh that. She said if she'd used his spoken name it might have been too obvious he was your father. Half the reason she acted hostile to James was she was really scared that, if his parents met you, they'd try to adopt you, to say she was an unfit mother as a promiscouos unmarried woman, and they would take you away.

"She may have been right, but it was terrible how she cut herself off from all the support she could have had. That was her way though. She'd never got good things from others since she was a little child. So she'd learned to trust almost nobody, even though she herself was kind to others in need.

"But sometimes, I wished she let others into her life more. It certainly have made her existence far easier. But I think the hurt ran too deep for her to change.

"As for her poor sister, I could never understand how your mother could blame a six-year-old who had no more control of her life than she did.

"I've never understood the thing about the man who was your grandmother's partner, but it seemed your mother had convinced herself he was looking after her mother, and her mother would have never died and the family wouldn't have been torn apart but for what her sister did. Even if Jane had a part, it seems a terrible thing for her to be blamed for what happened to the family when she was only six."

We talk for another half hour, filling in odd extra bits and pieces. Before we say goodbye, Linda tells me to ring her anytime if I want to ask more questions. After talking with her, I feel I've taken another small step towards understanding my mother.

It's too late to make a difference, but it matters to me how I remember her. I'm glad I know the truth.

Chapter 42 – Kate – Filling the Gaps

Jim has told me the story of my grandma and shown me her scrapbook and the other small remnants of her life. I'm grateful she did such a good job raising my father, despite her hard life. And I feel anger at the shameful way she was treated by so many people.

I've investigated what she wrote about her stepfather being a nice man, not hitting her mother. It's hard to get a clear picture, with the participants dead and a scanty written record from the court proceedings and adoption agencies. It was the 1950s when it all happened, a long time ago.

From my delve into history, it appears that my grandmother's mum served briefly as a nurse, caring for badly injured soldiers after the the Second World War. While doing it, she became addicted to morphine, which was widely used to treat the injuries of the soldiers.

After this, once she was discharged from her job, she found other odd bits of work in hospitals and stole morphine to support her habit. In the early days of her addiction, her parents supported her, despite her falling pregnant twice. Her parents also cared for her two girls. But when my great-grandparents were tragically killed in a car accident, the remaining family's lives fell apart.

My grandma took up with a man who, by all accounts, appeared a bit rough and, of course, they were not married. The neighbours, on the other side from Ellie's house, were highly religious people who said they disapproved of them living in sin and thought it would harm the little girls.

They made frequent complaints to the police about the man beating up the woman and abusing the children, even though there was no direct evidence to support this, and nobody else ever reported it.

One night, when they heard screaming, the neighbours called the police again. This time the police found my great-grandma with a range of injuries in a half unconscious state and my grandma and her sister crying and only half-dressed.

The partner said my great-grandma had been high on drugs and had fallen down the stairs. The girls were screaming about what had happened to their mother, and said he was trying to help her, even though she was full of drugs and screaming at him.

Police, assuming he'd assaulted her, arrested him.

Based on only the say so of the neighbours that he was abusing the mother and the children, the girls were taken away and made wards of the state. The partner spent several months in jail awaiting trial on the charges.

It's clear that the police never interviewed the neighbours on the other side, including Ellie's mother, even though they were close relatives. They were away for a few days on the night everything happened, and, by the time they found out, the girls had already been taken away and placed into care.

Nobody would give them the details of where the girls were or of the charges against the partner. My great-grandma didn't know what had happened to her children and, due to what had happened, she was deemed unfit as a mother, but she wasn't charged with any offence. She had no memory of the events of that night, or of how she got her injuries.

She was found dead in the house a few days later, the day before Ellie and her family returned. It was said she took a drug overdose. Perhaps it was suicide, perhaps an unfortunate accident. By this stage, the girls were fostered out with no reference to the rest of their extended family.

In the evidence tendered at the trial, my grandma, then only four, said that on that night, her mother's partner hadn't hurt her mother but had tried to help her. Jane, who hadn't seen what happened because she was asleep, couldn't offer any version of events.

The evidence of the girls was ignored in favour of the neighbours' story. Their tales of immorality in the household, along with their claims the man was abusing both the woman and her children, led to him serving five years in prison for assault. On release, he was barred from having any contact with the children.

Until her dying day, my grandma remained adamant that this stepfather figure was a good man, that the neighbours had lied, and that her older sister should have stuck up for him too, as he'd never hurt them or their mother.

After the man was released from jail, he went on to become a model citizen and had three children of his own. I located his oldest daughter, a woman in her sixties. She said that, until his dying day, her father was adamant he'd never hurt either the mother or girls, and that the whole thing was a fabrication. He wasn't angry or bitter, but wished he'd done a better job protecting this woman and her children.

I feel inclined to believe my grandmother and this man. Perhaps her life would have been different if others had believed them too. But this has become an accident of history that can't be undone and now almost seventy years have passed.

Still I'm very glad to have our house back and to have the real pictures to help me remember my grandmother and her family. I stay here for a night a couple times a month. When I do I use my grandma's old bedroom.

I love waking up on these mornings to a light filled view of the layered, flower gardens, which she too saw from that window. These views, along with the bird paintings, once greeted her every morning.

For me, it's like awakening to joy and colour to begin the new day. Each time I look out, both the view and the thought of Grandma seeing it too, gives me a thrill. I'm so glad this small part of her memory and her lost legacy still remains ours to treasure.

Of course, Jim is her legacy too, as am I. One day I hope to have my own child sleep in this room and so pass this continuing story on to another generation.

Of late, I've started seeing a man who feels like he could be the one, but it is too early to think about. He's very much a gentleman, and we've yet to be intimate, but I feel we're becoming more connected over time. I'm ready for that and more. Marriage doesn't really matter to me, but I'm determined that any child of mine will know both their mother and father.

As for Jim's house, there have been many discoveries in the last months. We found Michael, buried as expected alongside his aboriginal wife in the grave in the yard. In his grave, we also found a package with some papers that have helped fill in missing pieces of his history.

They include a letter from his other wife, Rose, written not long before her own death. In the letter, she says she's ill with a growing cancer inside her that will soon eat her up. In this letter, she tells Michael she loves him and thanks him for the happy life he's given her, for their children and so much more. But she also says she knows about the hidden secret of his past wife and family. She had found his diary when he was out with his brother, shearing sheep for the day at their farm in Ireland. She'd been looking in his room for a book to read, and had instead picked up the diary and began to read it. In this way, she discovered the story of his other, earlier relationship and his earlier children.

But she was in love with him and didn't want to allow him to go back to another, so she'd said nothing and redoubled her efforts to woo him and they had worked. She'd been sure that, once they married, he would always be a good and faithful husband and a good father to their children, and it had proved true.

When she knew she was dying and their own children were grown, she wrote him this letter to say that, after she was gone, she wanted him to return to find his first wife and children and set things to rights with them.

And so that is what he did.

It's clear from the stories in America, as told to Josephine, that his son, James, there never forgave this; he considered it was treachery to his mother's memory to go searching for another.

I suspect, in Michael's letters to his daughter, he must have told her the truth.

Without real facts, from there, the rumour of a black stain on the family from the father's deeds grew and gained currency. I don't really blame this family for any bitterness. It appears that once Michael left them he never returned and, apart from odd letters, he cut himself off completely.

By the time he returned to Australia, he was a wealthy man, having built three successful business ventures, first in Australia, then in Ireland and lastly in America. The house he built in Deepwater, America, was worth a large sum alone, and his papers also detailed the money he'd given to each of his three children there for their business ventures and also the properties he bought them and other wealth he left.

In all material ways, they were well provided for. But yet, after the death of their mother, they also lost their father too. If they were close to him, this must have been a cruel blow.

As for what Michael did after he left, he says he brought a suitcase of American dollars back to Australia, with an eye to finding his first wife and building a grand house for her to live in. It seems that, by then, he had ceased caring what others thought.

But what he found was an empty house, on a small plot of land. The rest of the surrounding land had been taken away from him and its aboriginal people to build the first railway running from Sydney to Parramatta.

At the time he returned, his own house was also slated to become part of this railway land. The government had been trying to find its owner to buy it but had been unable to do so, so it was left in place while the first rail track was laid around it, then a second track was laid on the other side, the original rail lines to Liverpool and Parramatta enclosing his land in a wedge.

Being the legal owner, on his return, he moved back into the house and set about finding his family. It took a month, but eventually, he found his son, Connor, now a man in his thirties and married with children of his own, living in a place at Elizabeth Bay. Connor took him to see his mother, Yura, and his two sisters, Maria and Angela.

They'd been moved to La Perouse, where they were in a camp for remaining Sydney aboriginals, being forced to vacate the house by the railway ten years before. Michael brought Yura and his daughters' home, and they lived on in his house between the railway lines until his death thirty-seven years later.

Soon after his return, his oldest daughter married a man from the North Coast of NSW, and she moved there to live with her husband. His youngest daughter had three children with a young Irish man from County Kerry named Patrick Keegan. Patrick died of tetanus when his hand was crushed in an accident a few years later, so Michael and Yura helped their daughter raise her three children, a boy and two girls.

As the children grew to adulthood, Michael used some of his vast sum of American dollars to help each one get their own house, this being an essential measure of prosperity in his eyes.

The two sisters married two Italian immigrant brothers, and Michael paid a large share of the costs for them to build two side by side houses in Redfern. The youngest son, Stephen, stayed on with his mother and his grandfather who taught him his trade of masonry, helping him set up his own business, working with stone mined from the quarries like his grandfather had done before him.

Yura only lived for a decade after she returned home, but they had been happy years as she watched her grandchildren grow, and she had taken delight in being with Michael again as he had with her. When her health was failing, she had asked to be buried in this place of her forefathers, the place of sweet water as it was called in her language, a preserved memory of the native wells nearby of her childhood.

Michael and Stephen carved the vault to place her in, alongside a small natural soak in back corner of their yard. They brought in large intact sandstone slabs from Pyrmont and, over months, they slowly made the intricate floral patterns and curved edge decorations of the vault. When Yura died, they laid her out in it with her aboriginal totem items to go with her to the dreamtime land, according to the custom of her people, where she lay undisturbed, until Michael joined her twenty-five years later.

Michael did not mention in his writing why he never uncovered the basement again with its hidden gold and other things, but a clue is there in the way he refers to what he knows happened in his brother Neil's family in Ireland, after he too died.

In a letter to his younger sister in Ireland he wrote, "The way they all squabble over his inheritance is unseemly. I'm glad I've given my American children enough to live a good life. From here it is up to them.

"I have done the same with my Australian children and grandchildren. But there will be no big inheritance when I die, nothing to fight over and destroy family bonds. The dollars in my suitcase from America are ebbing, most being used to pay lawyers to keep my house. It will be just enough to see me through to the end of my days, but that is all."

In my student's search of the early railway records, I uncover a set of letters between Michael, his lawyers and NSW Railways, who wanted to acquire his land for railway building. These letters fill in some more gaps.

Michael's argument was they did not need his land as the railway had already been built, running both sides of his house. The land his house was on was his land, to which he held a freehold title, so it was fine to stay as it was. It interfered with nobody, and he had an ongoing right to its continued enjoyment.

As time went by, more and more railway lines were built. First there was a duplication then a quadrupling of the lines, then more besides. In due course, the early lines next to his house were replaced with improved high-speed lines further away. At one stage there was a plan to use his wedge of land for more railway workshops, but other land had already been set aside for this purpose and his land was not needed.

Over two decades, these arguments continued between Michael's and the government's lawyers, each firing alternate salvos that resolved nothing. In the end, all the important development was done, the house remained in its tiny space, and the world moved on to other things. The railway records were buried in their archives, and all those people who remembered this battle had retired. So it gradually faded from living memory. For a century since the house had remained alongside two derelict railway lines, in the middle of other railway buildings, a relic of a vanished past.

When Michael died, Stephen buried him alongside his wife and carved the second inscription. He told nobody of this death, but had a document signed by Michael to ensure the land was transferred to him. By this time, he had built his own far grander house in Newtown and had moved there, though for a few years his daughter lived in the railway house, and then her own son lived in it between the wars until the Depression came, and he abandoned the house as he went off in search of work. Later, he enlisted in the Army where he died in a foreign battle. Before leaving Sydney, he passed the title deed to his aunt in Redfern for her to mind. Decades later, her own daughter sold it on to Jim.

Discovered in bits and pieces, we now know most parts of the story of my father and his antecedents, beginning with Michael and his aboriginal wife, Yura, our distant great, great, great grandparents. That mystery has been solved.

What I still do not know is the story of my mother.

I don't even know her surname. All I'm fairly sure of is the Cindy part.

On my birth certificate, issued by St Vincent's Hospital, I'm called Emily Martin, taking my father's name. My mother is named Cindy Lawler, not Lucinda McGrevy, the name Josephine knew her as.

So I think the name Cindy is right, though of course it may be Lucinda, even something else like Cinderella, princess of fairy tales, a girl of magic slippers, something like how I'd imagined her in my childhood fantasies. It could be another name again but to me Cindy feels real.

As for her surname, it could be either name, but neither feels like it really belongs. I suspect these names were merely things that she took and used. Perhaps she borrowed them from those who gave care, or names from school days. I don't feel as if either the Lawler or McGrevy name is hers and mine, though one of these names marks her grave. How am I ever to know?

Josephine never knew her best friends true name or antecedents. She didn't know Cindy's abusive adoptive parents, all she had was the name Cindy used at the brothel, and the story Cindy told her on their first meeting. Cindy never said where she'd lived or who her foster parents were. Based on Cindy's description, it sounds like they lived somewhere in south west Sydney, but that's no more than a wild guess.

I'd like to know more about her, the elusive Cindy who held me and loved me as a baby. All I have of her is a single photo and a locket with that name in, made in cursive script, on it, tiny fragments of almost nothing.

Most of my life, I've had a sense of searching for her.

Along the way, I've discovered another past, my father, Jim, and his new wife, Josephine, who feels like another mother. They and the descendants from my father's side are a whole new family, all of which gives me an amazing connection to this place.

I am happy and grateful for all these things.

But still this one mystery remains.

Who was Cindy? What was her story?

I'd like to know it if only to write an epitaph to go on her grave. I fear I'm destined to never know, that God alone knows, and unless he chooses to reveal her, Cindy will remain forever an eternal mystery.

Perhaps it's best it stays that way, to leave part of life's great mystery unsolved.

About the Author

Graham Wilson lives in Sydney, Australia. He's written and published twelve novels and a family memoir, *Arnhem's Kaleidoscope Children,* along with a range of combined novel box sets.

They comprise two series:

1. Old Balmain House Series – three novels

2. Crocodile Dreaming Series – five novels, and a two-book prequel

Risk Free, his previous novel, was released in 2019.

The *Old Balmain House Series* starts with the novel, *Little Lost Girl*, which was previously titled, *The Old Balmain House.* Its setting is an old weatherboard cottage, in Sydney, where the author lived for seven years. Here a photo was discovered of a small girl who lived and died 100 years ago. The book imagines the story of her life and family, based in the real Balmain, an early inner Sydney suburb, with its locations and historical events providing part of the story background.

The second novel in this series, *Lizzie's Tale*, builds on the Balmain setting. It is the story of a working class teenage girl who lives in this same house in the 1950s and 1960s. When pregnant, she is determined not to surrender her baby for adoption, and she finds herself struggling to survive in an unforgiving society.

The third novel in this series, *Devil's Choice*, follows the next generation of the family in *Lizzie's Tale.* Lizzie's daughter is faced with the awful choice of whether to seek the help of one of her mother's rapists' in trying to save the life of her own daughter, who is inflicted with an incurable disease.

The Crocodile Dreaming Series, based in Outback Australia, starts with the first novel, *'An English Visitor'*, which tells the story of an English backpacker, Susan, who visits the Northern Territory. She is captivated by and in great danger from a man who loves crocodiles. The second book, *Crocodile Man*, follows the consequences of the first book, after discovery of this man's remains. The third book, *Girl in an Empty Cage*, is about Susan's struggle to retain her sanity in jail while her family and friends desperately try to find out what happened on that fateful day. In *Lost Girl Diary,* Susan vanishes, and the book tells the story of the search for her and four other lost girls whose passports were found in the possession of the man she killed. The final book in the series, *Dance of Shadows,* is the story of a girl who appears in a remote aboriginal community in North Queensland, without any memory except for a name. She rebuilds her life from an empty shell and, as fragments of the past return, with them come dark shadows that threaten to overwhelm her.

The prequel to this series has also been published in two parts. It's the story of what made the central book character, Mark, becoming the person he was. Part 1 of this prequel, *Return of the Breaker*, tells part of the story of Mark's life, as written by him in a notebook found after his death. Book 1 tells how an abused boy survives a tormented childhood and grows into a charming but dangerous man, who forges his own uncompromising path through life, seeking to follow in the footsteps of the Breaker, that famous horseman who has become an Australian legend of many other books and films. The real Breaker lived and died a century before. His famous last words as he faced a firing squad at his execution were, "Shoot straight, you bastards." Mark seeks to live and die with similar courage.

The second part, the book, *'Whirlwind'*, completes Mark's life story. Its dark final chapters tell of a search for vengeance and retribution, which consumes him like a whirlwind, sucking him down, deeper and deeper into the worst of his own human nature. The Prequel is best read after other books in the Crocodile Dreaming Series in order to properly understand it.

Arnhem's Kaleidoscope Children tells the story of the author's life in the Northern Territory: his childhood in an aboriginal community in remote Arnhem Land, of the people and beauty of this place, and changes of the last half century with the coming of aboriginal rights and the discovery or uranium. It tells of surviving an attack by a large crocodile and of his working over two decades in the outback of the NT.

Graham is planning a memoir about his family's connections with Ireland called *Memories Only Remain* and is also compiling information for a book about the early NT cattle industry and its people.

He is also gathering stories set in the inner Sydney 'Rocks' area, where he, his wife and their three fluffy dogs live in one of Sydney's oldest houses. Many people have said to him, 'If only the walls could talk.' He hopes one day they will reveal some of their secrets.

Graham writes for the creative pleasure it brings him. He's particularly gratified each time an unknown person chooses to download and read something he has written.

He loves getting reviews, both good or bad. These give him insights into what readers enjoy and help him improve his writing.

In his other life, Graham is a veterinarian who works in wildlife conservation and across rural areas with landholders. He lived a large part of his life in the Northern Territory. His books reflect this experience.

More information about Graham and his books and writing is available from the following sites:

Graham Wilson – Australian Author on Facebook

Graham Wilson Author Profile on Goodreads

If you want to contact with Graham please email:

grahamwilsonbooks@gmail.com

www.ingramcontent.com/pod-product-compliance
Lightning Source LLC
Chambersburg PA
CBHW050015120726
47903CB00006B/1786

9780648311232